TORCH BIBLE COMMENTARIES

General Editors

THE REV. JOHN MARSH, D.PHIL.
Principal of Mansfield College, Oxford

THE REV. DAVID L. EDWARDS, M.A.
Editor, SCM Press

THE REV. CANON ALAN RICHARDSON, D.D.
Professor of Christian Theology in the University of Nottingham

FOREWORD TO SERIES

The aim of this series of commentaries on books of the Bible is to provide the general reader with the soundest possible assistance in understanding the message of each book considered as a whole and as a part of the Bible.

The findings and views of modern critical scholarship on the text of the Bible have been taken fully into account; but we have asked the writers to remember that the Bible is more than a quarry for the practice of erudition; that it contains the living message of the living God.

We hope that intelligent people of varying interests will find that these commentaries, while not ignoring the surface difficulties, are able to concentrate the mind on the essential Gospel contained in the various books of the Bible.

Volumes in the series include:

Already published
GENESIS I-XI, by Alan Richardson
DEUTERONOMY, by H. Cunliffe-Jones
RUTH AND JONAH, by G. A. F. Knight
ESTHER, SONG OF SONGS, LAMENTATIONS, by G. A. F. Knight
THE BOOK OF JOB, by Anthony and Miriam Hanson
II ISAIAH, by C. R. North
THE BOOK OF DANIEL, by E. W. Heaton
AMOS AND MICAH, by John Marsh
ST MATTHEW, by G. E. P. Cox
ST MARK, by A. M. Hunter
ST JOHN, by Alan Richardson
ACTS, by R. R. Williams
ROMANS, by A. M. Hunter
I CORINTHIANS, by W. G. H. Simon
II CORINTHIANS, by R. P. C. Hanson
GALATIANS, by John A. Allan

EPHESIANS, by John A. Allan
PHILIPPIANS AND COLOSSIANS, by F. C. Synge
I AND II THESSALONIANS, by William Neil
HEBREWS, by William Neil
JAMES, by E. C. Blackman
REVELATION, by R. H. Preston and Anthony Hanson

In preparation
GENESIS 12-50, by A. S. Herbert
EXODUS, by G. Henton Davies
I AND II SAMUEL, by D. R. Ap-Thomas
EZRA, NEHEMIAH, CHRONICLES, by Peter Ackroyd
JEREMIAH, by H. Cunliffe-Jones
HOSEA, by G. A. F. Knight
ST LUKE, by W. R. F. Browning
THE PASTORALS, by A. R. C. Leaney
I AND II PETER AND JUDE, by C. E. B. Cranfield
I, II, III JOHN, by Neil Alexander

THE FIRST EPISTLE TO THE

CORINTHIANS

Introduction and Commentary

by

W. G. H. SIMON

Bishop of Llandaff

SCM PRESS LTD
56 BLOOMSBURY STREET LONDON WC1

First published 1959

© SCM PRESS LTD 1959

Printed in Great Britain by
Northumberland Press Limited
Gateshead on Tyne

CONTENTS

Preface   9
Bibliography   11

INTRODUCTION

The world into which St Paul was born   13
The mission of St Paul   17
The background of Corinthian society   20
The background of Pauline thought   22
The Corinthian correspondence   26
The date of this epistle   28
The previous history of the Corinthian Church   29
The subjects discussed in I Corinthians   31
The significance and value of the epistle   33
Conclusion   48
Synopsis of the epistle   50

COMMENTARY

1.1-9   GREETINGS AND CONGRATU-
         LATIONS   59

1.10–4.21 DIVISIONS AND FACTIONS   63

1.10-17	What the Apostle has heard	63
1.18–2.16	True and false wisdom	64
3	The Corinthians' factious spirit reveals their spiritual immaturity	69
4	The apostolic task and responsibility re-stated	74
5	A BAD CASE OF IMMORALITY	78
6	LAWSUITS BEFORE HEATHEN COURTS	81
6.1-11	These are quite inconsistent with Christian behaviour	81
6.12-20	Why fornication is such a serious matter	83
7	A QUESTION FROM THE CORINTHIANS: MARRIAGE PROBLEMS	87
8–11.1	ANOTHER QUESTION: THINGS SACRIFICED TO IDOLS	95
8	Those who realize that idols are non-entities must not use their knowledge in a way that would hinder others	95
9	A digression: an appeal to the Apostle's own practice	98
10.1-13	The history of Israel affords a warning against spiritual pride	102

10.14-22	There is a real possibility of communion with the evil entities which the idols represent	105
10.23–11.1	Guiding principles on this issue	108
11.2–14.40	PROBLEMS CONNECTED WITH PUBLIC WORSHIP	110
11.2-16	The veiling of women	110
11.17-34	The Eucharist	114
12	What of spiritual gifts? and how are they to be exercised in public worship?	121
13	Charity	127
14	The Apostle returns to the question of spiritual gifts and their exercise	131
15	THE RESURRECTION OF THE BODY	138
15.1-11	The resurrection of Christ	141
15.12-19	Consequences of denying the doctrine of the resurrection	143
15.20-28	Christ's resurrection asserted as part of the divine plan	145
15.29-34	Further implications of unbelief	147
15.35-49	The nature of the resurrection body	149
15.50-58	What of Christians who survive until the Second Coming?	151

16   THE LETTER CONCLUDED   153

16.1-4   The collection for poor Christians
                at Jerusalem   153

16.5-12   Intended visits by Paul, Timothy
                and Apollos   154

16.13-24   Final salutations and exhortations   155

PREFACE

I Corinthians contains in chapters 13 and 15 two of the best-known passages in the whole Bible, and we learn from it and II Corinthians much of what is most attractive in the character of St Paul. There is, however, involved in these letters the complex problem of the whole correspondence between the Apostle and his converts at Corinth, which sometimes has a daunting effect upon both the would-be commentator and the student. But this problem has been handled, as well as possible in a commentary of this size, by Richard Hanson on *II Corinthians*; I have felt justified, therefore, in referring those interested in the problem to that commentary, which appeared in this series in 1954, and have contented myself with the barest mention of it. This, of course, is all the easier as I Corinthians differs from II Corinthians in being a harmonious whole, to such an extent that questions of interpolation or rearrangement are so subtle as to call for treatment only in a far more ambitious commentary than this one can claim to be.

I have worked throughout with the Revised Version and the American Revised Standard Version always at my side, and have found Fr Knox's *New Testament in English* of much help. Students will probably find the Revised Standard Version the most useful to follow. For the student acquainted with Greek, Moulton and Milligan, *The Vocabulary of the Greek New Testament* (1929), and Grimm-Thayer, *Lexicon of the New Testament* (1886; 4th ed., 1901), or Arndt and Gingrich, *A Greek-English Lexicon of the New Testament* (1957) are indispensable.

In addition to the books mentioned in the short bibliography I have consulted F. Prat's two volumes on *The*

Theology of St Paul (1949), R. H. Strachan's *II Corinthians* in the Moffatt New Testament Commentaries (1935), E. G. Selwyn, *The First Epistle of St Peter* (1946), J. Jeremias, *The Eucharistic Words of Jesus* (1955), as well as the relevant articles in *A Theological Word Book of the Bible*, edited by Alan Richardson (1950; cited as *TWBB*), and *The Oxford Dictionary of the Christian Church*, edited by F. L. Cross (1957). I am indebted to the Rev. A. R. Davies, of Llandaff, for much help with typing, and to *Province*, a magazine of the Church in Wales, in which some paragraphs of the Introduction first appeared, for permission to reproduce these.

Llandaff   ✠ GLYN LANDAV:
1958

A SHORT BIBLIOGRAPHY

Note: books marked * are cited by author's or translator's name only.

COMMENTARIES

A. ROBERTSON and A. PLUMMER (International Critical Commentary, 1914, cited as ICC).

*JAMES MOFFATT (Moffatt New Testament Commentaries. 1938).

*H. L. GOUDGE (Westminster Commentaries, 1903).

*E. EVANS, *The Epistles to the Corinthians* (Clarendon Bible, 1930).

TRANSLATIONS

American Revised Standard Version (1952, cited as RSV).

The New Testament in English, by R. A. Knox (1945).

Letters to Young Churches, by J. B. Phillips (1947).

OTHER WORKS

*KIRSOPP LAKE, *The Earlier Epistles of St Paul* (1911).

*L. S. THORNTON, *The Common Life in the Body of Christ* (1942).

*J. A. T. ROBINSON, *The Body* (Studies in Biblical Theology 5, 1952).

*A. J. B. HIGGINS, *The Lord's Supper in the New Testament* (Studies in Biblical Theology 6, 1952).

11

O. CULLMANN. *Early Christian Worship* (Eng. tr., Studies in Biblical Theology 10, 1953; cited as: Cullmann *ECW*).

*A. D. NOCK, *St Paul* (1938).

Students will find much useful information in the articles in *A Concise Bible Commentary*, edited by W. Lowther Clarke (1952). There is still much to be gained from W. M. Ramsay, *St Paul, the Traveller and Roman Citizen* (1895), and even from F. W. Farrar, *The Life and Work of St Paul* (1879), as well as from later works such as T. R. Glover, *The World of the New Testament* (1931).

INTRODUCTION

THE WORLD INTO WHICH
ST PAUL WAS BORN

St Paul was born about the beginning of the first century
AD and died sometime between 64 and 68. We know from
the Acts of the Apostles that he was a young man when
St Stephen was martyred in the early thirties of the century,
and that when he writes his letter to his friend Philemon he
can describe himself as 'your old Paul'. So he was born
under one of the wisest and greatest of the Roman Emperors, Augustus, and died under one of the worst of them,
Nero; in between had come the morose but efficient
Tiberius, the mad Gaius, called Caligula, and the strange
Claudius, sickly and odd, but able. During all these reigns
the Empire was on the whole well and wisely governed, and
it is worth noting that Nero was sufficiently popular in the
provinces for a sort of Asiatic Perkin Warbeck to turn up
after his death and have a considerable following. This
Empire was as haphazard as our own, and on the whole
the emperors aimed at leaving well alone and relying so far
as possible on local systems of government, whether
national, tribal or civic. Well settled provinces were administered by a proconsul; the proconsul of such a province
as Asia or Africa was a person of extreme dignity, corresponding in importance and largely in functions to the
Viceroy of India in the days of the British Raj.

Less settled areas were administered by legates, as was
Syria, the province in which Judea was situated; particular
districts such as Judea were administered by lesser officials
called procurators. The procurator of Judaea lived generally

at Caesarea. Communications throughout the Empire were
excellent, and it is worth while remembering that Julius
Caesar could get to Britain more quickly than was possible
afterwards until the middle of the Victorian era: peace and
order were well preserved, and everywhere in the civilized
part of the Empire the dominant culture and the common
speech were Greek, so that if you could speak Greek you
were in much the same position as an English-speaking
person is to-day; you could get everywhere and make your-
self understood. Finally, there was the Roman citizenship;
for those who were given this great privilege there was
security of life and justice; they could not be flogged; if
convicted in a provincial court of law, they had the right
of appeal to the Emperor; and if they were put to death,
it was by the sword and not by crucifixion. St Paul enjoyed
these privileges from birth (Acts 22.28).

In nearly every city of any size in the Empire there was
a considerable Jewish community, and though from time,
then as now, their general prosperity and financial dexterity
led to outbreaks against them, they enjoyed a considerable
measure of security and influence. St Paul's birthplace,
Tarsus in the province of Asia (Acts 21.39), was no exception. It was a city of great importance; situated about
twelve miles inland, below the lofty Taurus Mountains, it
was the starting point of the lumber trade, and a great
centre of traffic and commerce. It was a city where Greek
influence was dominant, but where the East was still very
much alive; Dio Chrysostom, writing in the following century, tells us (*Oration* 33.48) that women went veiled about
its streets. Like all Greek cities it had its gymnasium and
theatre, and was particularly noted for its school of Stoic
philosophy which had produced, in Apollonius of Tyana,
who was a contemporary of St Paul, and Athenodorus,
philosophers of wide repute. All this was very attractive,
but there was a bad side to it as well; its religion was of the
worst type of paganism mixed up with Asiatic luxury and

the worship of the Phoenician Baal; it boasted as its founder the effeminate Sardanapalus, on the base of whose statue Strabo records that there were written the words, 'Eat, drink and enjoy thyself, the rest is nothing'. So bad indeed was this side of it that Apollonius said that it was impossible for a philosopher to live there, and went away.

Here St Paul was born, probably of moderately well-to-do parents, with connections in Jerusalem sufficiently prominent for him to have knowledge of the inner councils of the Jews (Acts 23.16).

He certainly spent some of his early and impressionable years at Tarsus, and seems at this stage to have kept his eyes open and to have been an interested spectator of the common life of the city. Thus he remembers the veiled women he had seen as a small boy, and the importance attached to the custom (I Cor. 11.3-16); he had seen many a race in the gymnasium, and perhaps even run himself and boxed there, too (I Cor. 9.24-27); soldiers and their ways had fascinated him as they have other small boys before and since; and he had stood and watched with solemn eyes the building of houses and temples (I Cor. 3.10-13). The crooked way in which the merchants on the quayside did business had struck him: 'we are not going to haggle over or peddle the Gospel,' he says, 'we are going to deliver it in all its purity' (II Cor. 2.17). Or again, 'God has given us security here in the gift of the Holy Spirit of the full payment he is going to make hereafter' (Eph. 1.14). He seems to have hung about the theatre, and even perhaps the arena, where the 'acts'—and the spectators—became more and more bloodthirsty as the programme proceeded (I Cor. 4.9). To have allowed all this his father could not have been too strict a Jew, but still the time came when he felt things had gone far enough; perhaps the young Saul had begun to quote some odds and ends of the Stoic philosophy which he had picked up from acquaintances at the University of Tarsus. Anyhow he was sent at about fifteen years of age to study under Gamaliel at Jerusalem, where he had a married sister with whom he could stay.

The choice of Gamaliel throws light on the way in which St Paul had been brought up. Held in the highest repute, he was yet definitely on the liberal side in Judaism, was believed to be a student of Greek literature and favoured definitely friendly relations with non-Jews. But Gamaliel's immediate influence on St Paul was slight; the atmosphere of the holy city of his religion was too much for him, and he recoiled in horror from all thoughts of the paganism with which he had once been so familiar. Not for years afterwards did his boyhood in Tarsus and his learning from Gamaliel bear their fruit. Then, while not for a moment closing his eyes to the hideous vices of contemporary paganism, he was yet able to write to the Romans that even without the Jewish Law to guide them the Gentile world was led by God in the voice of conscience; then he would recognize the sincerity and pathos of the altar to unknown gods in Athens, and feel how clearly some Stoic phrases expressed the Being and Activity of God even though they did not realize it. But it was many years before he reached this view, and if his father in sending him to Jerusalem had wanted to convince him of the glory of his heritage as a Jew, then he completely succeeded. To St Paul, as he looked back on his life and considered his early advantages, whatever Greek civilization had had to offer him was entirely forgotten. It was his Jewish birth and upbringing, pride in his accomplishments as a Jew, thankfulness that he had been born a Jew, that he brings up again and again. And the great grief of his life, and one of his greatest puzzles, is that his people, the children of promise, have rejected the Messiah. It takes much of the joy out of the wonderful work God has enabled him to do. The highest praise that he can give to the Christian Church is to call it the New Israel; and the Jews from whom it sprang, without whom it would not have been possible, are that true remnant to whom the prophets had foretold God's promises. So Paul's 'heart's desire and supplication to God' for his people is not unanswered; there are *Jews* who have believed, just like the seven thousand long ago who had not bowed to Baal; and what will the glory of the Church be like when all God's chosen people have turned to it? St Paul is a Jew, heart and soul, and first and last; there is only one thing that he is anything like so proud of, and that is his Roman citizenship. Yet all, pride of race, pride of citizenship, pride of religion, he will sacrifice them all for Christ.

THE MISSION OF ST PAUL

The supreme crisis of St Paul's life came with his conversion on the road to Damascus (Acts 9, 22, 26). It was the turning point of his whole life. The actual event has been much debated. What did St Paul think of it himself? In his book, *The Meaning of Paul for To-day*, Professor Dodd writes: 'He was an enthusiast and a mystic, with powers of rapt contemplation beyond the common. He was also one who could apply the cold criticism of reason to his own dreams and assess soberly the true value of the more abnormal phenomena of religion.'[1] It will be worth our while, then, to notice what he thought of this experience himself. He believed that he had seen a vision of Jesus in risen and glorified humanity as objective as those seen by the original witnesses with which he classes it (I Cor. 9.1; 15.5-8). Whatever the psychological processes by which St Paul reached the moment of his conversion, it was none the less a call of God if the psychological preparation for it had begun long before; he is his own witness to the profound spiritual discontent he had found in 'doing the works of the law' (Rom. 7.7-25); the young man at whose feet Stephen's

[1] C. H. Dodd, *The Meaning of Paul for To-day*, 1920, p. 27.

B

executioners laid their clothes could not have been wholly
unmoved; the very violence of his persecution is testimony
to the doubts he thus strove to extinguish. But whatever we
may say or feel about the process, the fact remains: Saul
the Jew from that moment became Paul the Christian; he
never afterwards doubted the reality or the meaning of his
experience. To quote Professor Dodd again, 'He was dominated by a white-hot zeal for the truth of which he was
convinced as he was convinced of his own existence; and
more, by a personal devotion to the Lord Jesus, as he
habitually called the divine Person who, as he believed, had
spoken to him first on the road to Damascus and never
again left his side. That devotion was his religion, and it
controlled his thought and his life.' The supreme place of
this vision in his life appears all the more clearly in its true
significance when we realize how, as for instance in II
Corinthians, he is careful to resist all temptation to put forward the marvellous as a claim for belief in himself: he
will be judged by what he is and does, and the sole purpose
of his being at all, and the end of all he does, is that the
heavenly vision should not be disobeyed and that the vision
of the glory of God which he had seen in the face of Jesus
Christ should be revealed to all men through him; that
men, seeing his weakness and failings, should realize that
it was the power of Christ that made him able to do all he
did: the weaker he was the more he owed to Christ. 'I
must do a little boasting,' he writes to the Corinthians,
'though perhaps I ought not; I am proud of being the kind
of man I am—of being so weak that everything I have I
owe to Christ' (II Cor. 12.1-10).

But although St Paul's experience of Christ is so intense
and personal, we have no suggestion anywhere that his
preaching of salvation through faith in Jesus is in any way
an innovation, except only in relation to his views on the
law of Moses. The faith which he preached was the faith
which he shared with the whole Church. He was, however,

a missionary, who in his earliest days had been brought up in a non-Jewish city, and as such he did not hesitate to employ, in his commending of the Christian faith, the modes of thought and expression current in the religious world of his time (I Cor. 8.5). But he never loses sight of the rigid basis of Judaism, a basis of belief in the one true God, and all his reported speeches start with a summary of the Jewish origins of the religion which he preached (e.g. Acts 17.18-31 and 14.14-17; and cf. I Cor. 8.4). He was convinced, too, that this one true God was the God even of the worst of men, and that his task was to make known to all the love of God which Christ proclaimed. Consequently, whatever gropings there are in the Gentile world towards the light of truth must be made use of and developed. The heathen world knew, for example, the voice of conscience; St Paul would show it the law of Christ. Pagan thinkers believed that behind the world were spiritual forces; St Paul would speak to them of the Spirit. The heathen world spoke of 'gods many and lords many'; St Paul would reveal to it the one God and the one Lord (I Cor. 8.4-6). It spoke of and sought salvation; St Paul would bring it the true salvation. It knew of saviour-gods who died and rose again; St Paul would show it the crucified and risen Saviour. It knew the need of cleansing from sin and defilement, and of communion with the divine at the feast tables of its gods; St Paul would reveal to it 'one baptism for the remission of sins' and one altar of communion and fellowship with one living God (I Cor. 10.16-21). To 'become all things to all men', to use non-Christian religious terms for Christian ends, to 'baptize' all that is good in paganism, is a policy full of risks. But it surely was the right one, and surely it was safe in the hands of this man who was 'a Hebrew of the Hebrews', an uncompromising monotheist who could not, consciously or unconsciously, do anything which would involve surrender of the smallest part of his belief in 'one God the Father of all' and 'one Lord, Jesus Christ'.

'Tremble, you beautiful and chaste images,' wrote Renan, 'you fine gods and goddesses, tremble; see the man who will raise the hammer against you. The fatal word has been pronounced. You are idols' (see Acts 17.16 and I Cor. 8.4).

THE BACKGROUND OF CORINTHIAN SOCIETY

The Christians to whom I Corinthians was addressed lived in the great seaport on its narrow isthmus which was on the direct sea-route between Asia and Italy. Destroyed by Roman jealousy in 146 B.C., it had been refounded a hundred years later by Julius Caesar as a Roman colony. The new inhabitants would have been Latin-speaking Roman veterans, but it was not long before the new colony reproduced the features of the ancient city and became a cosmopolitan maritime city numbering by St Paul's day perhaps half a million people. The Roman veterans were soon submerged in a polyglot community, including many Greeks and predominantly Greek-speaking, but including, too, large numbers of Orientals, a considerable international if floating commercial population, and a large colony of Jews to whom would be attached not a few 'God-fearers', drawn for the most part from the more religiously-minded Greeks. But although Greek and Oriental influences were so strong in Corinth, it still had about it much of the air and setting of the Roman colony as which it had renewed its life. The main temple was connected with the worship of the Imperial Family and was dedicated to the sister of Augustus; the government was Roman; the official language was Latin and most of the first century inscriptions which survive are in that tongue. In such a town, St Paul as a Roman citizen would be as much at home as he was in Tarsus, and as independent. In religion and morals the Oriental influence was dominant; the worship of Aphrodite predominated and, bad enough in itself, was made much worse by the introduction into it of the cult of the Phoenician Astarte. By St Paul's day the great city had become proverbial for its luxury and immorality. If you wanted to describe clearly and briefly someone's completely abandoned and debauched life you said he was 'playing the Corinthian'. The population was, then, unstable and excitable, closely in touch with oriental religions and movements of an exotic and luxurious type, easily passing from ecstasy to degeneracy. Amongst the religions which bulked so large in the city's life many, such as that of Isis, gave women a special place, and when we add to this fact the presence of large numbers of temple prostitutes we can understand something of what lies behind St Paul's attitude to ' woman in church' in chapter 11 of this epistle (cf. 14.34). Just as his boyhood memories of relatives and friends shocked by the unveiled women of Tarsus left a mark on his thinking, so his knowledge of what paganism could understand by women priests, and what depths of licentiousness it could lead to, marked his approach to the place of women in the infant church.

This was, however, but one of the problems to which Corinthian religious activity gave rise. Religion was bound up with the very structure of society and dominated all civic functions; they were necessarily involved either in emperor-worship or in idolatry, and Corinthians converted to Christianity found themselves in great straits over the question of their relationship to such all-pervading social and civic occasions. Some called for total separation; it is *possible* that St Paul himself had thought of this solution in the letter which preceded I Corinthians; at any rate some of his converts thought or professed to think that he had, and in this epistle we see him dealing with the problem in chapter 10. It was the first great city in which he succeeded in establishing a Christian Church, and he, the Roman citizen, the Greek-speaking Jew, could not fail to have been

attracted by its character, at once Roman, Oriental, and
Greek, and by the fact that so many who would hear him
speak there would be, like himself, travellers and voyagers,
likely perhaps to carry with them to many places the words
which he spoke. His work there appears to have met with
immediate success, but it is possible that he did not
make sufficient allowance for the temperament and environment of these new converts, who misinterpreted what he
meant by Christian liberty. Misunderstanding his teaching
about Christian freedom from the demands of the Jewish
law and under the influence of their environment and their
manner of life before conversion, some of the Corinthian
Christians seem to have taken up a completely amoral
attitude and deplorable things happened. They almost seem
to have taken to themselves a kind of catch-phrase to express what they meant by their new-found freedom in
Christ, perhaps even a distortion of one of St Paul's own
phrases. 'All things are lawful' they seem to have claimed,
and St Paul may be referring to and refuting this claim in
I Cor. 10.23.

THE BACKGROUND OF PAULINE
THOUGHT

This question of the law is for St Paul a fundamental
one, bound up with the questions of sin and salvation. These
questions are not worked out in this epistle, as they are for
example in the letters to the Romans and the Galatians, but
we shall never understand what St Paul is aiming at as he
writes to the Corinthians unless we are continually assuming
their presence in the background.

The clue to what he means by sin is to be found in Rom.
7; for him it is always sin and not just sins. This makes it a
much bigger and more dangerous thing, what St John calls
'the sin of the world' in which we are all involved simply by

being human; it is something much bigger than men's little daily sins; these become important only because, insignificant as they seem, they are part of this tremendous thing that grips the world, and therefore even the smallest sins are always dangerous. Where does this evil come from? St Paul uses both Jewish and Greek ideas in trying to find an answer. From the Jews he gets the idea that sin came into the world 'through Adam's transgression' (Rom. 5.12; cf. I Cor. 15.22). From our point of view the important truth here is that we are all one; humanity is a whole, vitally linked together; no individual acts or suffers by himself— humanity as a whole is always involved.

From the Greek world (though many Jews, too, were familiar with this line of thought) St Paul gets the idea that the troubles of the world are due to evil spirits (Eph. 6.12). They have got hold of us in what St Paul calls ' our flesh': by this he doesn't mean our bodies, as the Corinthians, followed by many in Christian history, seem to have thought, but our whole lower nature. The truth which we must grasp here is that sin must be seen as a profound disorder of a spiritual kind which involves not only man but the universe as a whole: the most terrible mistake we can make is to underestimate it. The consequence of sin is that a great gulf has been created between God and man (I Cor. 15.50: cf. 1.21; 2.14; also Gal. 4.3, 8-10; Rom. 7.20-24). Here then is St Paul's first problem.

Allied to this, as we have already said, is the problem of *the law*. This was the great and sacred treasure of his race; he believed that the Jews had been specially chosen by God to receive it, and it is because of this that, next to his conversion and faith in Christ, his greatest cause of thanksgiving is that he was born a Jew. It is to this sacred law, then, that he turns for help in his struggle against sin, and it became his second great problem because it failed him. What he says, in effect, is that the law teaches him the difference between right and wrong, exhorts him to do the

one and forbids the other. Such is the perversity of human
nature that this makes the wrong all the more attractive; we
seem irresistibly drawn to what is forbidden, and again and
again we resort to it. At the same time, we know that the
law forbids it; a great struggle is set up in our hearts, and
the law turns out to be powerless to help us; it can only
repeat its warnings and threaten penalties, and this leads
the sinner to despair. Enabled by the law to see the difference between right and wrong, man receives from it no
power to overcome the sin into which he constantly falls.
Two grave perils for the soul result from this: either men
try to make up for their sins by being very strict about a
multitude of little observances and instructions of religion
(as the Pharisees often were), or they get a distorted view
of God, think of him simply as a stern law-giver or judge
and not as a loving Father, and grow further and further
away from him.

What is the way out of this impasse? St Paul's one absolute certainty in life is that Christ has done for him what
the law failed to do. He is for St Paul the one supreme
reality because ' in the face of Jesus Christ he sees the glory
of God revealed ' (II Cor. 4.6). He has little hope of expressing in words all that Christ has meant to him, and the
many concepts he uses—Justification, Propitiation, Reconciliation and the like—have provided Christian thinkers
down the centuries both with fresh inspiration and with
fresh problems. Perhaps the most expressive and powerful
of his metaphors is that of ' death ' and ' life '. This is inevitable because his experience is based on a historic person
who died and rose again: so St Paul and those who with
him would follow in Christ's steps must ' die ' to the world
and the things most dear to it, and ' rise ' to a new life
where Christ is all and in all, so that it is best described as
' life in Christ '.

The solution to his problems, then, is for St Paul absolute
trust and surrender to Christ. This is what the word ' faith '

really means for him; it is a word differently used by different New Testament writers, but for St Paul it means just this. By this surrender we unite ourselves to Christ, and with him overthrow the tyranny of sin and evil and pass through death to life. We must think once again of humanity as one living whole, with each individual representing it all in his life and works: and 'as in Adam all die even so in Christ shall all be made alive'. It is true that this life-in-Christ is not perfect and complete now, for the Christian life must be lived among un-Christian surroundings, but it begins here and now with our surrender to Christ.

What did all this mean for the Jew and the Gentile of St Paul's day? For the Jew it meant a new view of the law and of his Scriptures, which we now call the Old Testament. They were now seen as a stage in the divine scheme, given for the guidance of the nation during its childhood, as it were. They still had much to teach men, but if they were proclaimed as God's final word, or if obedience to the law were set forth as the way of salvation in the place of surrender to Christ, then they became a positive danger. Of course St Paul did not reject the law; he believed that if only for the sake of his brethren a Jew should continue to observe it, and he rigorously observed it himself. Obedience to the moral law is still essential; but if the follower of Christ finds himself failing to obey it, he will not try to put it right by a still more earnest attempt to carry out its exact details, but will turn in repentance to Christ, receive God's forgiveness through him, and be given fresh strength for renewed struggle.

For the Gentile, St Paul's teaching meant salvation from a pessimistic view of the world and all material things as somehow tainted with an incurable and fatal evil, to be escaped from at all costs, alien to the things of the spirit. This attitude had the apparently contradictory consequences for would-be spiritual men of either an exaggerated asceticism or gross licence: either you treated the body and everything to do with it as something alien and gross or you held that as it was something completely transient and unrelated to reality, it did not matter at all what you did with it. For the Christian, on the other hand, the body is the instrument of the spirit, a shrine of the Spirit of God. The material world is the creation of the good God. This is one reason why St Paul stresses the resurrection of *the body*: Christian immortality is not just the immortality of the soul: as the body in this world is the means of expression of a human soul, so it can be the means of expression of that same soul in the world to come, though not as it is now. 'We shall be *changed*' says the Apostle in I Cor. 15.

Judaism, then, as a means of salvation, was finally put on one side, and the principles of God's universal father-hood and salvation for all, *through faith in Christ*, accepted. We cannot doubt that St Paul was right, or doubt that without him the spread of Christianity would have been much delayed and very different in form. But we may see, too, the truth in the position of those Jews who opposed him. They felt that the law was part of the final Divine revelation, and that without it there could be no security for the pagan convert. They feared that lacking the ethical and moral background which the Mosaic law had so firmly established for the Jew, the Gentile converts would either speedily lapse, or else introduce into their new community the lax moral standards and principles of the society from which they sprang. There was every danger that to preach 'freedom from the law' would be to secure not liberty but licence. Certainly the Corinthian Church was to provide some justification for their fears.

THE CORINTHIAN CORRESPONDENCE

St Paul must have written much that has been lost for ever and it is certain that our two letters are only part of his correspondence with the Corinthian Church. There is a reference, for example, in I Cor. 5.9 f., to an earlier letter laying down some moral precepts which seem to have been misunderstood. This letter has disappeared, though some think that a part of it has been bound up in our II Corinthians (II Cor. 6.14–7.1). Next in order was our I Corinthians, written partly to answer some questions asked by the Corinthians themselves in a letter brought by some of their members, and partly to deal with grave disorders there of which he had verbal information and about which the Corinthians in their letter seem to have said nothing. I Corinthians, however, did not settle matters, and it looks as if St Paul had to pay a personal visit (looked forward to in I Cor. 11.34) which was a failure owing to a move by a person or persons directed against his own apostolic authority (II Cor. 12.21). This seems to have been followed by a third letter which was taken to Corinth by Titus; it was stern and severe, and apparently succeeded in its purpose of bringing about an improvement. This letter is referred to in II Cor. 2.4 and 7.8, and is thought to have survived in part as 10.1–13.10 of our II Corinthians. On receiving the good news from Titus St Paul then wrote a fourth letter (II Cor. 1-9 and 13.11-14) full of joy and happiness. If this is a correct description of the epistolary course of events, then our I Corinthians is the second in a series of four letters from the Apostle to the Corinthian Church. The reconstruction we have given is, of course, conjectural, but can be reasonably defended and may be studied more fully in the Commentary on *II Corinthians* in this series by Richard Hanson or in the Moffatt Commentary on the same epistle by R. H. Strachan. So far as I Corinthians is concerned, there seems no reason to doubt that it is a harmonious whole as it stands, and attempts to find in it interpolations or embedded fragments of other letters have had little serious support.

THE DATE OF THIS EPISTLE

We have the account of the founding of the Corinthian Church in Acts 18, and we are able to connect it up with two events in Roman history, the expulsion of the Jews from Rome under an edict of Claudius, which may be dated AD 49, and the term of office of Junius Annaeus Gallio, brother of the philosopher Seneca, as Proconsul of Achaia, which we know to have been 52-53. We learn from Acts 18.1 that St Paul left Athens for Corinth and met there a Jew of Pontus named Aquila and his wife Priscilla. They seem to have been already converts to Christianity, and, we are told, had only lately come from Rome in consequence of the Claudian decree referred to above. We may then reasonably assume that St Paul arrived in Corinth in AD 50 and stayed with Aquila and Priscilla, working at their common trade of tent-making and holding disputations in the synagogue, and later, when the Jews became hostile, in a near-by house. Whatever his original intentions he became divinely assured (Acts 18.9 f.) that he must stay in Corinth for a considerable period because much success would attend his preaching there. This he proceeded to do, despite the hostility of the Jews, who in 52 took the opportunity of a change of consul to try and get him either silenced or removed, by bringing him before Gallio on a trumped-up charge of illegal preaching. The attempt came to nothing; St Paul stayed on some little time longer, but during 52 or early 53 he left for Ephesus, where he remained for the best part of three years. Some time, then, during the period 52-56 he wrote his letters to the Corinthian Church. Nearer than this we cannot get with any certainty, nor is it particularly important that we should. We may, however, say that our I Corinthians was probably written during AD 55[1].

[1] For a different view, see Richard Hanson, *II Corinthians*, p. 11 n.

THE PREVIOUS HISTORY OF
THE CORINTHIAN CHURCH

St Paul's preaching of the gospel at Corinth was blessed with success, which must have been all the more encouraging to him after his disappointment at Athens and the hostility he had experienced in Thessalonica. He was fortunate from the first in having the companionship of Aquila and Priscilla. After a period of disputations in the synagogue on rabbinical lines, his claims for the Messiahship of Christ were uncompromisingly asserted after the arrival of his companions, Silas and Timothy, from Macedonia. This, as always, aroused acute Jewish hostility and he transferred his activities, plainly not in any spirit of compromise, to a house next door belonging to Titus Justus, probably a Gentile and possibly a Roman of some standing, with leanings to Judaism. It is just possible that his full name was Titius Justus Gaius, and that he is the person referred to in I Cor. 1.14 as having been baptized by St Paul, and in Rom. 16.23 as 'my host, and the host of the whole church'. Although the converts included 'the ruler of the synagogue', Crispus and his family, and other households like that of Stephanas, the majority of the converts were no doubt Gentiles (Acts 18.8: 'By now many of the Corinthians listened and found faith and were baptized'). It was now that St Paul felt himself divinely guided to make a stay of some duration at Corinth in the confidence that God was promising him 'a great following in this city'. It is a sign of the success which attended his work, and of the fact that it was by no means confined to Corinth, that the greetings with which II Corinthians begins include 'all Christians throughout Achaia'. Certainly by the time the Epistle to the Romans was written there was a church at the port of Corinth on the Saronic Gulf, Cenchreae. Nor was the work checked when St Paul left. It was, in fact, to have a fresh

impetus after his departure. His friends Aquila and Priscilla had met at Ephesus an Alexandrian Jew named
Apollos, an eloquent and able speaker, deeply versed in
rabbinical knowledge. He is said, when he met them, to
have ' known only the baptism of John ', by which phrase we
may reasonably understand that he had been baptized by
John the Baptist or a disciple of his, and had accepted the
urgency of the Messianic preaching but had not, probably
through lack of opportunity, gone further and recognized
Jesus as the Messiah whom John foretold. At Ephesus he
received further instruction from Aquila and Priscilla
and then crossed over to Corinth with the support of
the Christian community there, to continue St Pauls'
work of evangelization, which he did with powerful
effect.

It is possible to see from the account in the Acts of the
Apostles and from the Corinthian correspondence itself
that Christianity must have ' got off to a good start ' in
Corinth and numerous converts must have resulted. Most of
its membership would have come from the working-classes,
dockers, foundrymen, the smaller tradesmen, sailors, passing travellers, clerks, freedmen and slaves, and also a certain
number of higher social standing like Crispus and Gaius,
and women obviously of some position in the city like Chloe
and Phoebe. But it was not long before developments
showed that the success had come too quickly and that if
the church at Corinth was to survive and grow along the
right lines, much further instruction would be needed. Even
half a century later, as we may learn from Clement of Rome,
the Corinthian Church continued to be liable to excitement,
strife and instability, and our Corinthian correspondence
shows that this presented St Paul too with urgent problems. After Apollos had left Corinth, news soon reached
the Apostle that things were not as they should be. The
difficulty seems to have been involved with moral questions;
Christians were too ready to associate with people whose

conduct was far from what it should be and to countenance
by their company behaviour incompatible with their Christian profession. St Paul wrote them a letter of considerable
severity. It is referred to in I Cor. 5.9 f., and seems to have
been interpreted to mean that he was calling upon them to
have absolutely nothing to do with men of bad character.
Obviously, he says, I did not mean that, for to do that ' you
would have to cut yourselves off from the world altogether;
what I meant was that if any *Christian* were to fall into
conduct of that kind you must not seem to condone it by
continuing to associate with him '. It does not look, then,
as if this first letter had achieved its object, and it is with
the developments subsequent to this that our I Corinthians
is concerned.

THE SUBJECTS DISCUSSED IN
I CORINTHIANS

These fall into two groups, those which were raised by
the Corinthians themselves and those raised by St Paul,
about which they had been silent. It may well be that in ' a
somewhat effusive letter ' as Moffatt calls it, they brought
forward a carefully selected set of problems in the hope
that the Apostle would either be distracted from or never
hear of others about which they could reasonably expect him
to be both grieved and displeased. We can work out a fairly
accurate picture of the Corinthian queries from St Paul's
answers to them, which may be found in the sections intro-
duced by the words ' Now about ' this, or that; viz. 7.1-40;
8.1-11.1; 12.1-14.40; 16.1-4; 16.12. Their queries would,
then, have been concerned with marriage; their relation to
heathen sacrifices and the implications of these in their daily
life; problems connected with spiritual gifts and their exercise; the church collection for Jerusalem; and a possible
further visit from Apollos.

The points raised by St Paul himself, to which the Corinthians had made no reference, may be found in 1-6; 12.2-31; and 15. From these chapters we learn that there were serious divisions in the church there. Not only were there splinter groups, giving themselves out as followers of Paul or of Apollos or Cephas, with some disdaining all these and claiming either to be more spiritual, or to be recipients of a direct revelation. These last claimed to be 'Christ's party': we are reminded of 'The Disciples of Christ', the title taken to themselves by nineteenth-century American followers of Robert Sandeman. There were also more serious divisions based upon claims of some members to be specially spiritual, to have their own 'philosophy of religion' and to want the Gospel preached in terms of lofty eloquence and refinement, with the underlying suggestion (made with open hostility by the time II Corinthians was composed) that St Paul had not appreciated all this. This spirit of strife had so permeated their relationships one to another that they thought nothing of taking petty little disputes to be settled in heathen law-courts. We learn, too, that St Paul had heard of grave moral disorders, involving fornication and incest, about which the Corinthians had shown considerable complacency.

Just as they had kept silence about this sort of thing while asking gravely about marriage difficulties, so, while asking about 'spiritual gifts' they had said nothing about disorders at worship, and worst of all, had concealed abuses in connection with the Eucharist itself, which was dishonoured not only by gluttony and drunkeness but by a complete lack of charity. As if all this were not enough the Apostle had heard that some of them were denying that 'dead men can be resurrected'. 'There are some of you,' he says, 'who say there is no resurrection.' There is nothing surprising about this. 'The Apostles and their converts,' wrote A. E. Taylor in *The Faith of a Moralist*, 'were not primitive savages . . . who had never bethought themselves that a resurrection from the dead is a startling departure from the primitive routine.' Possibly a minority even denied the resurrection of Christ himself, but this hardly seems likely. What was troubling the Corinthians was the matter of the resurrection of themselves and their departed friends. Just as the Fourth Gospel was later to stress that in a real sense eternal life is here and now (although of course the Evangelist was never in any doubt about the *fullness* of that life being something beyond our grasp in this world), so Christians, with St Paul himself, saw themselves as 'dead and buried with Christ in baptism' and 'risen to new life with him (Rom. 6.1-4)'. Was not this, some no doubt felt, what was meant by the resurrection life? What was all this about 'bodies'? Was anything necessary beyond a belief in the immortality of the soul, to which so many intelligent men assented? Such a belief would certainly have fitted in well with the views of the 'spiritual' party in the church and of those who placed their confidence in 'the wisdom of this world' and were, in all the churches he founded, to give St Paul such trouble.

THE SIGNIFICANCE AND VALUE OF THE EPISTLE

'A brilliant inconsistency' is how Wilfred Knox once described I Corinthians, a letter in which the Apostle 'deals with the disorders which had arisen out of a perfectly logical interpretation of his own teaching'. It is just here that we see the first sense in which I Corinthians has made a permanent contribution to the well-being of the Christian Church. It is largely concerned with the application of Christian principles to particular situations, and it is small wonder that more than any other of his letters it was widely read and as widely referred to from the earliest days. This is no doubt primarily because he is dealing in it with what

is often called ' practical Christianity ', Christianity as it is
worked out or as its relevance is sought in particular situations in which the majority of us find ourselves sooner or
later. There is a real possibility, as we have seen, that St
Paul was taken by surprise by the Corinthian interpretation
of Christian liberty and by their failure to grasp the incom-
patibility of Christian moral teaching with the environment
to which they had been accustomed. But it would be a mistake to suppose that, as Wilfred Knox's phrase suggests, he
now had to improvise on a large scale. Much, indeed
most, of what he says in this letter could only have been
said if he could assume a knowledge of Christian principles
already imparted to them. What he had to do was, partly, to
explain how these principles worked in situations where the
Corinthians had failed to find the answers, or in other situations where they had failed to see that the principles were
involved at all. Wherever human beings exist in society
some of these situations will always arise; sexual problems,
the break-down of marriage, the vocation to the celibate
life, these are ubiquitous in varying degree. It may be
that the Apostle, full of the sense of urgency that his
expectation of the imminent Second Coming gave him, and
disappointed by the distractions or failures that marriage
sometimes brought in its train, takes here a less happy and
lower view of marriage than we would have wished. (If he
is the author of Ephesians he put this right later). But this
does not lead him to unbalanced views of celibacy; he
recognizes that there are two vocations, to marriage and to
celibacy, and would certainly be on the side of those who
to-day see amongst the causes of marital breakdowns in-
adequate teaching about marriage on the Church's part,
and too hasty and light-hearted an entry on it. There is
nothing unbalanced, either, about his attitude to sexual life
within marriage, and he sees clearly the dangers of an over-
ascetic approach to it and the damage its suppression can do.

We must recognize that St Paul, with the first Christians

in general, expected the return of Christ within a short time
after the ascension. Such must be the meaning of passages
like I Thess. 4.13–5.11 : 'The dead in Christ shall rise first.
Then we which are alive that are left shall together with
them be caught up in the clouds to meet the Lord in the
air.' The same sense of urgency may be detected in this
epistle (see, for example, 3.13; 7.26 and 29; 16.22) and he
shares the same vocabulary of fire and clouds and trumpets
and assize. But we see him in the later epistles using this
vocabulary less and less, as he re-interprets the thought
associated with Christ's Second Coming. There is more and
more emphasis on the divine community, the Christian
Church, and its significance in the world, a growing realization of the decisive importance of the coming of the Holy
Spirit and his indwelling in the Church, a closer approach
to the Fourth Gospel's re-assessment of the whole eschatological hope in terms of the Spirit. The question of the actual
date of the Second Coming recedes more and more into the
background, a process which we can trace—as, for example,
in Mark 13.32, or Acts 1.7: that day is known 'only to the
Father' and 'It is not for you to know the times and
seasons'. What remains is the certainty that 'that day'
will come, and the consequent sense of urgency that must
beset the Church. Christians are living in a time of crisis:
how long, in human terms, that time may last is secondary;
it must be seen in the light of eternity. By the time of II
Peter this was realized and 'scoffers' who ask 'What has
become of the promise that he would appear?' are told
that 'the Lord is only giving you more time, because his
will is that all of you should attain repentance'; and the
faithful are told to bear in mind that 'with the Lord a
thousand years are as one day'. Until that day comes it
must be enough for them to know that 'they will receive
power from the Holy Spirit', for this Second Coming is
essentially connected with the re-creative work of the Holy
Spirit, and the spiritual activity so evident in the Christian

community is an 'earnest, a pledge' of the full revelation of divine power which he is to bring about. It is the Spirit who is the link connecting the believer with Christ, making him a participator in Christ's resurrection (Rom. 8.5-11). It is the Spirit who by his indwelling gives life to our mortal bodies (Rom. 8.11). It is the Spirit who in the Church gives faith in the saving acts of Christ which took place in the past, gives hope for the return of Christ in the future, and gives realization to both in the present through his action in the Eucharist. It is these saving acts of Christ, and above all, his resurrection, which have already brought in the New Age; 'history has reached its fulfilment' in them (I Cor. 10.11). There can be no hope in the future act of Christ which is not based upon faith in his acts in the past. Christ has already come, the powers of darkness *have been* defeated, 'death hath no more dominion' over the Christian (Rom. 6.9). The final issue is not in doubt, but sin and death have not yet been abolished. Their power has been broken, but they have yet to be crushed. Hence, all the centuries since Christ have been 'eschatological', 'the end-time, the time in which in the Church the decisive and final moment of the death and resurrection of Christ develops'.[1] We are in the final phase of the divine plan revealed by the gospel, and the note of urgency sounded by the early Church, and not least by St Paul in this epistle, must be always contemporary and related to the particular age in which the Church lives. If not, 'the trumpet' will give 'an uncertain sound' and none 'will prepare themselves for the battle'. In the particular age in which we live, when at least the material destruction of the world we have known is an ever-present possibility, this note of urgency seems particularly relevant. The fact that it is on the whole absent from the Church's preaching may well be judged to be not unconnected with its admitted ineffectiveness.

'Meats offered to idols' (ch. 8) seem, at first sight, to have

[1] Cullmann, *The Early Church*, 1956, p. 155.

little to say to our condition, but the kind of problem they represent is immediately and literally contemporary in the mission-fields of the Church, and it would be foolish to suppose that the principles the Apostle lays down for the Corinthian Christians as they tried to live a Christian life in the middle of a non-Christian society have nothing to say to us. At what point does 'broadmindedness' pass over into weak compromise? To what lengths can we carry toleration of practices which are wrong, or of conduct which is un-Christian, without its being supposed that we condone it? We may well find it impossible, as the Corinthians did, 'to keep no company with fornicators' when we have to mix in society with people who make no pretence of obedience to Christian precepts. But what of our attitude to those who within the community have broken the seventh commandment or transgressed our Lord's directions about marriage? To what extent may we be sure that the money we earn is not polluted at the source by association with un-Christian purposes? If we hold shares in some company or other, are we sure that the objects for which our money is being used are wholly, or even primarily, Christian? The observance of solemn seasons of the Church, such as Holy Week and Good Friday, or of festivals such as Christmas, is becoming increasingly secularized, or they are treated as primarily social occasions. To what extent should we be prepared to stand aloof from, or how far may we fall in with this tendency, without compromising our Christian witness? Sunday recreation, and still more, Sunday labour, present problems which baffle many Christians of the mid-twentieth century; their bewilderment might be less if they had studied and made their own the advice which this epistle gives to their Corinthian forerunners in the Faith.

But it would be a great mistake if we supposed that the chief value of I Corinthians is that it 'marks the beginning of Christian casuistry', important as this aspect of it is. St Paul throughout relates the 'practical' advice he is giving to the doctrinal foundations from which he starts and on which he hopes to build. Thus the Corinthian disunity is wrong because it involves a denial of the essential unity of all Christians in Christ, and failures of charity derive their significance from the still greater failure to recognize their dependence on one another as 'members of Christ'. The 'sins of the flesh' are for Christians acts of utter disloyalty because they have learnt that since Christ died 'upon the tree' their bodies are no longer theirs alone, but his, and that the Holy Spirit of God lives within them as within a sanctuary. Striking out on one's own in this direction or that is not only foolish behaviour on the part of a very young and new church; it is a failure of the members to recognize that they exist as a church at all, not because they have thought they would like to be Christians, but because God has called them to himself through Christ in the power of the Holy Spirit to be members of the Church which already exists as the Mystical Body of Christ in the world. It is this tendency to isolationism which reveals that they have lost sight of the truth that Christian freedom is never individualistic; it is freedom in fellowship; and this imposes restraints and responsibilities if it is to survive at all as liberty in any real sense of the word. Libertinism, not liberty, awaits not only the individual Christian, but also the church which seeks to live 'on its own'. Of this fellowship in Christ the Apostle is the representative in all the churches, and it is in virtue of his apostolate that he exercises authority in the Church, giving directions, administering rebukes, setting in order, administering and ruling. This is an epistle in which one is very conscious of the one holy catholic and apostolic Church from which the local church derives its significance and existence. It is also an epistle in which doctrine and morals are closely interwoven; 'no Christian doctrine, no Christian morals', might well describe its message. Nowhere is this more clearly seen than in the great chapters on the gifts of the Spirit, of which charity is at once the beginning and

the end. It is not surprising, then, to find in this letter great
and specifically doctrinal statements; on the meaning of the
Cross, on the origins and significance of the Eucharist, on the
centrality of the Resurrection. These are explicit statements,
but throughout the epistle doctrinal assumptions are made
which are neither defended or expounded because a body
of common teaching can be taken for granted. Notice, for
example, how, as naturally and almost incidentally as in
Phil. 2.6, the pre-existence and cosmic functions of Christ
are referred to in 8.6—'for us . . . there is only one Lord,
Jesus Christ, the creator of all that is, who is our way to
the Father' (cf. 10.4 and John 14.6). Again, the atoning and
redeeming significance of the death of Christ is referred
to as part of the common knowledge of those to whom he is
writing: e.g. 'Has not Christ been sacrificed for us, our
passover?' (5.7); 'Have you never been taught that your
bodies belong to the body of Christ? . . . You were ran-
somed at a great price' (6.15, 20). Similarly, St Paul can
take for granted that the personal activity of the Holy Spirit
is a familiar concept; he is no mere emanation, but is personally active within the Church, giving spiritual gifts to
each 'as he will' (12.11) and in 2.11-13 the Spirit is able to
teach us the meaning of God's gifts, because 'he understands God's thoughts'; he is within the Divine Being.
Finally in 12.4-6 profound theological thought underlies the
Apostle's teaching about the essential unity which is the
foundation of the immense variety of the gifts and functions
to be found within the Christian Church. This unity in
diversity is naturally found there because the Church rests
upon the Being of God, where the same principle is plainly
to be discovered. 'Different kinds of gifts . . . but the same
Spirit who gives. Different kinds of service . . . but the
same Lord we serve. Different manifestations of power . . .
but the same God behind them all.' Once again we notice
how naturally and incidentally he can use language of this
kind, as if it were familiar to all, and how such language

never takes away from what 'early Greek theologians called the Monarchy of God the Father: whenever St Paul in this Epistle uses the word " God " it is the Father who is always intended.' It is God who is to be 'all in all'. (See Goudge, Introduction, pp. xxix-xxxi; and note on 15.28 in this commentary.) To those then who may welcome this epistle as concerned with 'practical' Christianity and devoid of the 'tedious dogmatics' of Romans or the 'rabbinical subtleties' of Galatians, it will be salutary to discover how firmly each piece of practical advice and direction is tied to its appropriate theological principle. Not the last part of its relevance and value lies just here, in its insistence that right beliefs hold the key to right conduct and that the Christian will find in his creed the sign-posts that mark the way to heaven.

The vital connection between doctrine and life is nowhere more clearly seen than in the life of the Church. This is indeed primarily a church epistle, and nowhere else in the New Testament do we get so much insight into the life of the Christian community as here. Baptism, for example, is simply taken for granted, not only as a *fact* in the life of the Christian as in 12.13—'we have all been baptized into one body by the power of one Spirit'—but also as of doctrinal significance as in 6.11—'you have washed away your sins; you have been justified; you have been sanctified . . . by the Spirit of God.' All this was in accord with St Paul's own experience of baptism by means of which he had 'been filled with the Holy Spirit' (Acts 9.18 f.). Only the most perverse exegesis can see in this Epistle (1.14) any slighting of the significance of baptism: 'I thank God I baptized none of you' is nothing more than the ejaculation of a justly incensed pastor.

The commentary which follows will be treating of the place and significance of the Eucharist at the appropriate points and here it will be sufficient to note that this epistle takes its centrality for granted. It is the Christian passover

(5.7) and there is at it a real partaking of the Lord's Body and Blood (10.16 and 11.27); it is at once a commemoration and a proclaiming of his death in the context of his coming. 'In the Eucharist Christians collectively and individually make (as it were) the Sacrifice of the Cross their own act . . . and maintain and deepen their fellowship with God through Christ.'[1] The celebration takes place in the context of a common meal reproducing the Last Supper. All bring to this their own contribution, which is shared with all.

We read also of teaching, some of it corresponding to what we mean by a ' teaching sermon ' (12.8), but some of it rather the result of a special insight or inspiration. There are Psalms, and there is a free use of what we would call ' extempore prayer' by different individuals as they were moved (12.7-11 and ch. 14, esp. 26-end). There are, too, stereotyped liturgical formulae like the Amen and the *Maranatha* and the Grace (16.22-4; cf. II Cor. 13.12 f.). The whole picture is one of a combination of freedom and liturgical forms at work side by side in a way no longer produced satisfactorily, through deficiency in one element or the other, in either Catholic or Protestant worship. The aim of it all is ' the building-up of the community . . . not in the hackneyed pietist sense of "uplift"; we have to think of the figure of the *body of Christ*, which must be formed effectually in the community '.[2]

When we turn to the organization of the Christian community we find, as we should expect, that it is still rudimentary and on the whole undefined. But the list of what we should call ' officers ' in 12.28 ff. at least leaves us in no doubt of the place of the Apostles, not here limited to the twelve: it is ' Apostles' who come first, as in Eph. 4.11. ' Prophets', too, are much to the fore, but although it is obvious that, like the Apostles, they form as it were a class, the gift of prophecy is not limited to them precisely because

[1] ICC, Introduction, p. xiv.
[2] Cullmann, *ECW*, p. 26.

it *is* a gift, a gift of the Spirit, and not an office; a gift which is plainly bestowed on some, but may be bestowed on all (14.31) like other charismatic gifts. The apostolic office is in a different category from this; he who holds it exercises a definite authority which has been bestowed on him and is by no means bestowed on all. Although very little is explicitly said in the epistle about the meaning and scope of apostleship, much can be gathered from St Paul's comments on particular situations and the plain inference of much of what he says. Note, for example, the tone of authority in 4.17-21. His is the power of discipline—'Shall I come to you rod in hand?' (4.21)—and it is in complete accord with this that he lays down the procedure for excommunication of a notorious sinner and directs that it is to be carried out (5.4 f., 13). Christ is the supreme authority for the Church, and where there is a 'word of the Lord' the issue is settled, as in the case of marriage (7.10), but where there is no such word, because, for example, the particular circumstances involved had not arisen in Christ's ministry, the Apostle himself acts with authority, directing, defining, instructing, and that not only in Corinth, but generally (7.12, 17). This apostolic authority is not something individualistic or personal, for he is careful to make it clear when he is giving a personal as distinct from an apostolic direction (7.40), even though he may believe his personal opinion to be based upon divine guidance.

It is this sense of apostolic authority in the epistle which leads us directly to the source from which it comes, the Church of God. For it is the Church of God which is the recurring theme of this epistle. We must not be misled by the use of the plural 'churches' (as in I Cor. 7.17 and 14.33) or by such a phrase as 'everywhere in every church' (I Cor. 4.17) into supposing either that 'the Church' is divided into 'churches' or that 'the Church' is formed by the uniting of 'the churches'. We must look for the origin of the Pauline (and New Testament) word for Church—the

ecclesia—in the Septuagint, where it denotes the holy congregation, the People of God, Israel. For St Paul, consequently, the word means 'the whole Church', the whole
congregation, the New Israel, the new People of God; each
local community is this whole Church in miniature, and
into the People of God each new Christian is incorporated
at baptism. By reference to the faith, the morals, the
worship, the teaching, even the ritual, of the whole Church,
the life and practices of each local gathering of the People
of God must be tested and approved or condemned, a concept which did not come easily to the Corinthians with their
inherited Greek tradition of individualism, faction and de-
bate (see I Cor. 14.33, 36 f.). They are warned to 'give no
occasion of stumbling, to Jews or Greeks or to the Church
of God' (I Cor. 10.32) and St Paul's apostolic authority, they
are reminded, is derived from God, but through this one
Church, for 'in the Church' God has set 'first, Apostles'
(I Cor. 12.28), the very Church of which he had been at one
time a persecutor (I Cor. 15.9), and which, in their attitude
to its poor members, the Corinthians are unconsciously
despising (I Cor. 11.22). Nowhere is this essential dependence of the local church upon the whole Church more
clearly brought out than in the words of greeting at the
beginning of this epistle: the Corinthian Church is here
saluted as 'the Church of God, as it is at Corinth'. It is
the same relationship which is in view in the title of the
English Prayer Book which is described as 'The Book of
Common Prayer . . . and other Rites and Ceremonies of
the Church, according to the Use of the Church of England'.
Behind all is the conception of the one Church, the
Church of God, who calls whom he will to be numbered
with 'his saints, with all that call upon the name of Lord
Jesus Christ in every place' (I Cor. 1.2). Thus it is that the
Church is formed, and not by the coming together of in-
dependent groups attracted to one another by similar ideas
about worship or order or ways of belief; it is this divine

origin of the one Church in the one God that is the true
foundation on which Christian unity must be built and the
true reason why Christian disunity is a 'scandal' (in the
New Testament sense of that word as something which
causes a man to stumble on his way to God).

Accustomed as we are to various adjectives qualifying
the word 'church', it ought to be all the easier to grasp
the significance of the fact that St Paul qualifies it only by
the words 'of God' or 'of Christ', except in this epistle
(14.33), where we have the phrase 'all the churches of the
saints'. (This need cause no surprise, since at I Cor. 1.2 the
ecclesia is identified with 'them that are sanctified in Christ
Jesus'.)[1] The significance of the one Church is to be seen
not only in the light of God, but of God in Christ. As there
is but one God, so there is but one Christ, and divisions in
the one Church are, as it were, a tearing in pieces of the one
Christ, a breaking up of his one Body.

These words bring us to one of the great Pauline contribu-
tions to the theology of the Church, his development of
the idea of the Church as the Body of Christ. Attention will
be called to this concept where it is present or implied in
this epistle at appropriate points in the commentary, and a
full study of it may be found in such books as *The Common
Life in the Body of Christ*, by L. S. Thornton, or *The Body*,
by J. A. T. Robinson; see also A. M. Ramsey, *The Gospel
and the Catholic Church*.[2] Meanwhile we may note that it
is in this epistle that we get the idea first definitely put
forward (chapters 6 and 12). No doubt it was an idea that
appealed strongly to St Paul from his own experience on
the Damascus road, when he saw Christ and his persecuted
followers as one, and he was to draw out the implications
of it and fill them with grandeur and wealth of meaning in
the epistles which he wrote from his prison in Rome. But

[1] See K. L. Schmidt, *The Church*, Eng. tr. (Bible Key Words) 1950,
p. 12.
[2] 1936, reprinted 1956.

the way in which he introduces the theme here for the first
time shows that he was not dealing with anything novel or
strange. The very words of the Eucharist had made it
familiar, and the closing words of the Parable of the Sheep
and Goats in Matthew, and the Allegory of the Vine and
the Branches in John, show that it was a theme known in
the Church at large. But it is St Paul who brings it out and
develops it, and we shall not understand his treatment of
it if we see it merely in terms of a metaphor or simile or
think of the word 'body' in terms of the modern use of it
as denoting a society or group of which one can be a
member. When the Apostle calls the Church 'the Body of
Christ' he means that the Church *is* Christ himself in his
own being. To be 'in the Church' is to be 'in Christ', 'in
Christ Jesus', a phrase which Sanday described as 'one of
the pillars of St Paul's theology'. Into this Church we are
incorporated by baptism; we are grafted into it as a branch
is grafted into a living tree. This is primarily a Johannine
approach; St Paul's is different, but the result is the same.
'In one Spirit we were all baptized into one body' (I Cor.
12.13): 'as many of you as have been baptized into Christ
have put on Christ' (Gal. 3.27). This incorporation means
that Christians share as living parts of his Body in all the
work of Christ. They are partakers of his passion and death
and they are partakers, too, of his resurrection; through
them the saving power of Christ's redemption is applied to
all to whom the gospel is preached in the Church's journey
through human history, in the ages since the saving act of
God in Christ was seen and known in time and space
(Col. 1.24 f.). In the Church the Christian lives, in Christ,
through the bread and wine of the Eucharist, and it is the
life of Christ there received which makes possible the unity
of Christians, despite all their infinite variety: for 'Is not
the bread we break a sharing in the body of Christ? The
one bread makes us one body though we are many in
number; the same bread is shared by all' (I Cor. 10.16 f.).

Through the Eucharist the Church, and the Christian born into the Church by baptism, shares in the passion, knows the joy of the resurrection, and eagerly awaits the return of her Lord.[1]

'For as the body is one and has many members, and all the members of the body, though they are many, yet are one body: so also it is with Christ. We, too, all of us, have been baptized into one body by the power of a single spirit, . . . you are Christ's body, and individually members of it' (I Cor. 12.12 f., 27). It is the work of the Spirit which brings into being and gives life to the Church as the Body of Christ. Life in the Church is life in the Spirit, and it is in the power of the Spirit of God 'who raised up Jesus Christ from the dead' that Christ gives himself to his own in the sacraments of Baptism and Eucharist, the means of grace, the media through which the Spirit works. 'You shall receive the power of the Holy Ghost coming upon you, and you shall be witnesses to me; there is a baptism with the Holy Ghost which you are to receive, not many days from now' (Acts 1.5-8). So it was that the little band of faithful followers were 'born again' at Pentecost and received their new life in the Church of Christ. Their natural birth 'in Adam', i.e., as men in the order of nature, was a birth that came to its end in death; their spiritual birth 'in Christ', i.e., as men in the order of grace, is a birth to endless life. For 'as in Adam all die, even so in Christ shall all be made alive.' 'The Spirit is the instrument by which the substance of the resurrection hope, the risen body of Christ, becomes ours and quickens the bodies of those who are in Him' (Robinson, p. 72). For 'if the Spirit of him that raised up Jesus from the dead dwelleth in you, he that raised up

[1] See Cullmann, *ECW*, pp. 33 f., and especially 'The Lord's Supper is the climax to which [every Christian gathering for worship] moves . . . since here Christ unites himself with his community as crucified and risen and makes it in this way one with himself, actually builds it up as his body'; and compare II Cor. 4.10, 11, 14 and the relevant notes on ch. 11 in this commentary.

Christ Jesus from the dead shall quicken also your mortal bodies through his Spirit that dwelleth in you' (Rom. 8.11). It was this possession of and by the Spirit that most decisively marked off the New from the Old Israel: it was the fulfilment of the prayer of Moses (Num. 11.29): 'Would God that all the Lord's people were prophets and that he would put his Spirit upon them.' In the Church no man could rightly lay claim to *exclusive* gifts of the Spirit. Gifts differed, but they were given not for individual glory, but for the 'building up of the Body of Christ'. Some of these spiritual gifts were dramatic, even sensational, but the greatest of them gave a new quality and meaning to life and belonged, as the others did not, to the Eternal Order. Life 'in the Spirit' was as truly found in what we may by an anachronism call 'liturgical worship' as in the 'extempore' prophesyings, prayers and 'speaking with tongues'. St Paul would have had no difficulty in teaching the Corinthians the Johannine formulation of eucharistic doctrine: 'This is the bread which came down out of heaven: not as the fathers did eat and died: he that eateth this bread shall live for ever. . . . It is the spirit that quickeneth; . . . the words that I have spoken to you are spirit, and are life.' (John 6.58, 63). It is in the normal religious acts of daily life that these words bear their fruit, for these are created and sustained by the Word-made-Flesh, present in the eucharistic worship of his Church, which draws its life from the bread and the cup through which it shares in the life of the risen Christ, and maintains itself in the world as his Body. 'On him all the body depends; it is organized and unified by each contact with the source which supplies it; and thus, each limb receiving the active power it needs, it achieves its natural growth, building itself up through charity' (Eph. 4.16). Hence the Christian community is the natural home of supernatural graces; there are to be found the 'fruits of the Spirit', sometimes indeed striking and arresting, serving particular needs or special ends, but

always those whose presence marks the growth of the
Christian life ' in Christ '; ' love, joy, peace, patience, kind-
ness, goodness, faithfulness, gentleness, self-control, faith,
hope, charity ' (Gal. 5.22 f.). In St Paul, then, we deal with
no isolated or individualistic Christian but with one to
whom, if we may be adjectival as St Paul was not, membership of the one Church, holy, catholic, apostolic, is an ever
present reality, on which his Christian profession depends.
What epistle could be more relevant for Christians in a
century which has seen so remarkable a revival of the sense
of the Church as the Mystical Body, but has seen, too, so
strong a revival of non-Christian values in Christian lands,
and so great an upsurge of hostility to the Christian religion
amongst people still to be won for Christ?

CONCLUSION

It was with all this in his heart that the Apostle went
about his calling, proclaiming the gospel as the Spirit gave
him utterance, so that ' not only in Jerusalem and Antioch,
in Athens and in Rome, but in every place the faith of Christ
is spread abroad '. Rome and Corinth, Thessalonica and
Galatia are the four names which stand out for us, for they
are connected with the four great epistles—the Rome
of Nero, of Gallio, of Petronius Arbiter, the elder Pliny and
Seneca, where the old virtues and the old religion, personified a century before in Marcus Cato, had already begun to
seem quaint, and were now quite out of date; Corinth, as
notorious in the popular imagination for vice and wanton-
ness as Paris once seemed to solid middle-class Englishmen;
Thessalonica, over which still moved the shade of Alexander, where Rome and the East met one another on the great
Egnatian Road; Galatia, where the Gaul and the Greek
had hardly influenced the life, the language or the mind of
the Persian and the Mede. It was a time in which for the

Roman and the Greek the old gods of hearth and city had lost their meaning; when the solid domesticity of the Roman and the confident rationalism of the Greek had given way; when there was, in Gilbert Murray's well known phrase, a 'failure of nerve', a sense of insecurity in the world, a groping in a world that seemed quite capricious after something more stable, after a hope of sure salvation—a hope and a feeling which the new worship of Rome and the Emperor did little to satisfy. Men were 'through the fear of death all their lifetime subject to bondage'.

Into this world, sailing in its cockleshell boats across the tempestuous seas, climbing its mountains, striding over its plains, shut up in its prisons, haled before its magistrates, greeted by its multitudes, stealing through its stinking streets and alleys, moving amongst its crowded slave population, living at last in Rome itself, came a small, sturdy, not very attractive Jew,[1] who spoke Greek which everybody could understand, and was a citizen of that Empire which gave him peace and swift means of movement. Dauntless, but often despondent, enthusiastic but often despairing, he passed unnoticed by most of the world; but here and there a man or woman had been touched, and in Corinth and Ephesus and Antioch and Rome itself, and in scores of other cities, little groups were burning as separate fires, soon to join together in an irresistible blaze, kindled by the faith of this Jew that he held the secret of the hopes of all mankind: the God whom without knowing they revered, he could show them; he had the means to save them from fear, to give them security; he could give the Jews their sign and the Greeks their wisdom. Now he might pass unnoticed, or be haled to prison and to death; but he knew what he believed and he knew who inspired him; he preached Christ crucified, to the Jews a stumbling block and to the Greeks foolishness, but, to them that believed, Christ, the power of God.

[1] So the second-century apocryphal work, *The Acts of Paul and Thecla*.

D

SYNOPSIS OF THE EPISTLE

1.1-9   Greetings and congratulations.

DIVISIONS AND FACTIONS

1.10-17   The Apostle has heard about the growth of parties within the Corinthian Church.

1.18–2.16 True and false wisdom.

3.1-4   The Corinthians' factious spirit makes it necessary for St Paul to deal with them only in very elementary terms on such subjects.

3.5-17   Perhaps a metaphor from gardening or building operations will help to make things clear.

3.18-23   If they do not grasp this truth, they miss the heart of the Christian gospel.

4.1-5   St Paul restates his apostolic task and responsibility.

4.6-13   The Corinthians' self-satisfaction has obscured this from them.

4.14-21   It is therefore his apostolic and fatherly duty to recall them to unity and humility.

IMMORALITY

5.1-8   A shocking case, which, if it goes unpunished, will have ill effects throughout their community; severe measures must be taken.

5.9-13   Bad company outside the Church cannot always be avoided, but within the Church it must be shunned, and the sinner responsible removed.

LAWSUITS BEFORE HEATHEN COURTS

6.1-4   Such remedies are completely inconsistent with the high calling of the Christian Church.

6.5-7   It is better to suffer grievous wrongs than to try to put them right in this way.

6.8-11   But the Corinthians, far from submitting to these wrongs, even inflict them upon each other; and despite their baptism they have failed to recognize the gravity of sins of the flesh.

6.12-20   Above all, they have failed to see how by fornication they are wronging Christ himself; for their baptism has made them members of Christ, and temples of the Holy Ghost.

A QUESTION FROM THE CORINTHIANS ON MARRIAGE

7.1-9   The right use of marriage. The Apostle himself thinks celibacy better, but marriage is a vocation too; sex has its rightful place, and those who feel they are called to marriage must answer the call.

7.10-16   Divorce is forbidden to the Christian; this is Christ's own precept. In particular cases arising in connection with 'mixed marriages', the Apostle's personal view is that separation may be desirable.

7.17-24   But this does not involve remarriage. In general, God expects Christians to live in whatever walk of life or condition they may find themselves when he calls them.

7.25-38   These general precepts must guide fathers anxious about the desirability or otherwise of marriage for their daughters.

7.39 f.   This applies also to widows considering remarriage.

ANOTHER QUESTION: THINGS
SACRIFICED TO IDOLS

8.1-6   It is true that idols are non-entities, and there-
             fore that to share in what is offered to them is
             meaningless.

8.7-13   But not all have reached the stage of realizing
             this; and those who have must not, in self-
             sufficient pride, act in such a way as to mis-
             lead others.

9.1-14   St Paul too has his rights, as an Apostle.

9.15-27   But he has decided in the interests of the
             gospel not to claim them.

10.1-13   There are very real dangers in spiritual pride,
             and the example of their Hebrew forefathers
             in the faith provides a salutary warning that
             mere participation in the sacraments will not
             save them from the consequences of it.

10.14-22   They must also remember the evil entities
             which the idols represent; there is a real possi-
             bility of communion with such beings at the
             sacrificial meals, and this must at all costs be
             avoided by Christians who share in the
             eucharistic food.

10.23-11.1   The guiding principles must be: everything
             we do or leave undone must be to the glory
             of God and for the well-being of our fellow-
             Christians. This is to follow Christ, as St Paul
             himself seeks to do.

A DIGRESSION: THE APOSTLE HAS BEEN
HEARING ABOUT DISORDERS IN
WORSHIP

11.2-15   Unveiled women are a scandal at worship; they
             offend against divinely appointed principles of
             order in creation.

11.16   Such singularity, whatever support it may find in Corinth, is clean contrary to the practice of the Church.

11.17-22   The social distinction, selfishness, greed and drunkenness which have been allowed in connection with the Meal of Christian Fellowship, can only have arisen because the Corinthians have forgotten the solemnity of the Eucharist with which it is associated.

11.23-26   This has come down to us by divine command.

11.27-32   Their conduct will have the gravest consequences, not only spiritual but even physical.

11.33 f.   It must be put right at once; the Apostle will look further into the situation when he visits them.

A QUESTION ABOUT SPIRITUAL GIFTS: HOW ARE THEY TO BE RECOGNIZED? AND HOW ARE THEY TO BE EXERCISED IN PUBLIC WORSHIP?

12.1-3   A sure way of differentiating between good and evil spirits is by the question, 'What is their attitude to Jesus?'

12.4-11   However varied spiritual gifts may be, there is an underlying unity, as they all come from the same Spirit.

12.12 f.   This unity of the Spirit is the vital principle of the Church, the Body of Christ, of which we are all members by baptism.

12.14-26   The analogy of the human body will help us to understand this.

12.27-31   Diverse as the gifts of the Spirit are, however, they are of varying value, and Christians must desire the highest of them.

13.1-13   Greatest of them all is charity, which the Apostle will now expound to them.

14.1   Charity must be the regulative principle, but
            there are other gifts which may rightfully be
            sought.

14.2-5   Two of these are prophecy and speaking with
            tongues. Of these there can be no doubt that
            prophecy is superior and more to be desired,
            for it is intelligible and seeks to build up the
            Church.

14.6-17   Speaking with tongues, undoubted gift of the
            Spirit though it is, is essentially incommuni-
            cable.

14.18-25   St Paul possesses it in no small degree, and
            thanks God for it; but he values more highly,
            and so must they, those gifts of the Spirit which
            edify the Church and instruct others.

14.26-33   Even in spiritual things, order and discipline
            must be observed; there must be no jostling
            or interrupting one another in the use of
            these gifts, and if there is to be speaking with
            tongues, it must be a private affair, unless
            there is someone present to explain what is
            said.

14.34-40   There is no place for feminine activity in all
            this, for it is contrary to church custom. Order
            is all.

THE APOSTLE UNDERSTANDS THAT
THERE ARE DIFFICULTIES AT CORINTH
ABOUT THE RESURRECTION, AND HE
PROCEEDS TO EXPOUND THE SUBJECT

15.1-11   He sets forth the accepted teaching of the
            Church.

15.12-19   He points out the consequences of denying the
            resurrection.

15.20-28   He expounds the divine plan, of which the
            resurrection of Christ is the first stage.

15.29-34   Both the practice of baptism for the dead, and
            the trials the Apostle himself is willing to
            undergo for the gospel's sake, imply a belief
            in the resurrection.
15.35-49   He explains, with the aid of similes from the
            natural order, the nature of the resurrection
            body.
15.50-57   He asserts the final victory of the Christian
            through Christ. For him, life and not death has
            the last word.
15.58   Here is the foundation for their confidence, and
            the motive for perseverance in the good life.

CONCLUSION

16.1-4   He gives instructions for the collection for the
            relief of poverty in the Church at Jerusalem.
16.5-9   He expresses his intention of visiting them.
16.10-12   Mention of suggested visits by Timothy and
            Apollos.
16.13-24   Concluding commendations and greetings.

COMMENTARY

I

GREETINGS AND CONGRATULATIONS

1.1-9

1.1-3. The usual epistolary greeting of the time (an example may be seen in Acts 23.26) is expanded in view of the particular situation which will be dealt with. The sender's standing and authority in the Church are emphasized; the addressees are reminded that they are not an isolated unit but part of the 'Church of God' and that the nature of their calling demands personal holiness; and the apostolic blessing brings to them not only God's free and loving favour but also the peace of which this divided church is so much in need. The word 'apostle', linked up with the idea of the apostolic ministry, has for some time occupied a prominent place in discussions amongst Christians, but as yet without full agreement. In the New Testament there is more than one usage of the word. In general it means one 'sent forth' and usually with authority to act on behalf of someone else (Luke 6.13). In Acts the word is used primarily of the Twelve Apostles (including Matthias) but it is also used of Paul and Barnabas, and that there was this wider use of it we may see from this epistle (15.5 and 7) where St Paul, telling of the traditional teaching about the Resurrection, says that the risen Lord appeared TO THE TWELVE . . . THEN TO ALL THE APOSTLES. From this epistle, too, we learn (12.28 f.) that to be an Apostle means to be the holder of the highest office in the Church. So far as St Paul was concerned it means one whose ministry

was divinely commissioned, an 'essential ministry' in the
Church. It is obvious both that the special position of the
Twelve must be something that ceased to exist when the
last of them died, and also that the kind of apostleship to
which St Paul believed himself called, to be an ambassador
for Christ, to preach the gospel, to edify the Church, to
exercise the ministry of reconciliation, to be a steward of
the mysteries of God, must always have its place in the
Church. Through the mists of the centuries we may dimly
perceive how this was secured by the appointment of
'presbyters' (as in Acts 14.23) who were entrusted with
solemn duties (as in Acts 20.17-36). (See also Phil. 1.1
where we hear of 'bishops' and 'deacons'. Lightfoot in
his commentary on Philippians identifies bishops with
elders and describes them as 'owing responsibility to a
superior power' and as 'absolutely essential to the existence
of a church and forming the staple of its ministry'.) The
exact course of the development of this ministry is concealed from us for a time after the end of the New Testament period. It passes from our sight, as has been said,
like a train entering a tunnel. But the tunnel is not a very
long one. In II Tim. 2.2 we find the author giving this
direction: WHAT YOU HAVE HEARD FROM ME BEFORE MANY
WITNESSES, ENTRUST TO FAITHFUL MEN WHO WILL BE ABLE
TO TEACH OTHERS ALSO. It may be that this is inserted 'by
a later hand', but hardly one later than the end of the first
or the beginning of the second century, and in the Pastoral
Epistles generally we see Timothy and Titus as 'apostolic
men', a link with the Apostles in their standing in the
Church. In the *First Epistle of Clement*, addressed to the
Corinthian Church about AD 96, and often reminiscent of
St Paul's own correspondence with that church, we are on
firmer and clearer ground than we are in the Pastorals.
Thus in chapters 42 and 44 we learn that 'the Apostles . . .
appointed . . . their first converts . . . to be bishops and
deacons of the future believers.' And this apostolic practice

is stated to be 'in accordance with good order and with the will of God', for 'the Apostles were from the Christ and the Christ from God'. 'We consider therefore that it is wrong for us to remove from their ministry those who were appointed by them, or later on by other eminent men, with the consent of the whole Church.' A short generation later, Ignatius is writing, 'Jesus Christ, our inseparable life, is the will of the Father, even as the bishops, who have been appointed throughout the world, are by the will of Jesus Christ' (*Ephesians* 3.2). The Church that emerges from the tunnel does not look so very different from the Church which entered it. The same notes of apostolic authority, of unity, of doctrine, of sacramental life, that we heard in the Corinthian correspondence, may still be heard. We may grant that the original Apostles were *sui generis*, that they stood to the revelation and to our Lord in a necessarily unique relationship that could not be transmitted; but this does not mean that we cannot also reasonably hold that such of their authority and functions as could be transmitted were indeed so transmitted. The little local churches of the post-apostolic years were like the one at Corinth; they did not come spontaneously into existence. The faith, the sacraments, the ministry, were *sent* to them; they did not make them for themselves. They received them from above; they were not infant ecclesiastical democracies; an apostolic authority was exercised over them; they existed by right of being parts of the one catholic and apostolic Church.

Sosthenes

A convert of whom we know nothing. He *may* have been the unfortunate person who was beaten up after Gallio's dismissal of the case against Paul (Acts 18.17).

4-9. The Apostle begins with words of thanksgiving and praise for what has been achieved in Corinth, but the things he specially mentions are not without significance. KNOWLEDGE and SPIRITUAL GIFTS are among their causes for satisfaction and pride, and St Paul alludes to the fact that for their perfection these gifts depend upon their Author and his grace.

5. Later St Paul has to criticize severely the inclination of the Corinthians to attach too much importance to the GIFT OF TONGUES, and indeed to eloquence generally, and to warn them that their boasting of their possession of a superior form of 'knowledge' was full of dangers through the spiritual pride that it engendered. But we must not underestimate the genuine spiritual attainments of the Corinthians or the enrichment which their wayward genius brought the infant Church.

8. The day of our Lord Jesus Christ.

Thus early we find mention of a major preoccupation of St Paul and his converts—the Second Coming of Christ. As we shall see, the thought of this coming event affected all their lives, and their attitude to every problem that confronted them.

9. God . . . Jesus Christ our Lord.

Here too we meet one of the recurring themes of the epistle, the essentially corporate life of the Christian because of his special relationship with Christ. ICC paraphrases thus: 'God . . . who himself called you into fellowship with his Son and in his Son, Jesus Christ our Lord.' Christians share the life of Christ, and as each one of them is IN CHRIST by virtue of his baptism, they also have a common life which they share with one another. Cf. I John 1.3: THAT YOU MAY HAVE FELLOWSHIP WITH US; AND OUR FELLOWSHIP IS WITH THE FATHER, AND HIS SON JESUS CHRIS.

II

DIVISIONS AND FACTIONS

1.10–4.21

WHAT THE APOSTLE HAS HEARD

1.10–17

News has reached St Paul from a reliable source, news of strife and dissensions, impossible if they thought on the source of their calling, Christ himself. (It was evidently in preparation for criticism of their party spirit that St Paul had so early written of their fellowship in Christ [v. 9].) The Christians mentioned by name in vv. 14-16 were no doubt of some standing in the community, but we know little of them except by conjecture.

12. Apollos

We learn of him in Acts 18.24-8. A Jew of Alexandria, MIGHTY IN THE SCRIPTURES, a follower of John the Baptist (see p. 30), his meeting with Aquila and Priscilla in Ephesus had led to what we might call a 'follow-up mission' in Corinth which had evidently been very successful. As an Alexandrian he may have been familiar with and skilled in the allegorical interpretation of the Scriptures; and this, with his eloquence of speech, would have made him an attractive teacher in Corinth. But there is never the slightest sign of any difference between him and St Paul, rather the contrary (see 2.6 f.); and in 16.12 he is reported by the Apostle as being by no means in a hurry to accept an invitation from the Corinthians to visit them again.

I of Christ

Perhaps not a separate party (though II Cor. 10-11 may indicate that such a party had developed by then), but either those who claimed to be ' spiritual men ', recipients of direct revelation, or possibly people who wanted ' no man to come between their souls and God '.

14. I baptized none of you

There is no contrast intended here between the ministry of the Word and of the Sacraments, and certainly St Paul must not be thought to be minimizing the importance of baptism. He has been baptized himself; he takes it for granted as an essential part of the Christian heritage (see e.g. 6.11; 10.2; 12.13). A right understanding of his teaching about baptism and its effects would have made impossible these party-allegiances; Christ is One, and they all one in him; how can he be divided up, as their actions suggest? Moreover, at the very moment St Paul is dictating this ironical passage he remembers two whom he baptized, and is, perhaps by the person taking it down, reminded of a third, Stephanas, all well known to the Corinthians.

TRUE AND FALSE WISDOM

1.18–2.16

In v. 17 St Paul has just declared that God has not sent him to preach the gospel with an orator's cleverness : people would then have been occupied with him rather than with the Cross. In vv. 18-25 he may be thinking of his own ineffectiveness at Athens, when he had attempted to supplement the plain preaching of the Cross by arguments suited to the taste of his audience, who, like the Corinthians themselves, were looking out for the kind of things contemporary philosophy had sunk to, a popular sophistry, intellectual fireworks, all sound and no meaning (vv. 19-22). Little wonder that when the Cross was preached in all its stark simplicity, neither Jews nor Greeks could appreciate it; in their different ways they all approached it from this world and its standards, whereas its origin lay in God and was part of the divine plan. The very nature of the Cross itself, the obscurity and lack of talents of those who preached it, the undistinguished character and position of those who responded to it, all alike emphasized its source in God, and the utter dependence on him of both preacher and convert (1.23–2.5). GOD'S POWER, NOT MAN'S WISDOM, WAS TO BE THE FOUNDATION OF YOUR FAITH (2.5, Knox). They should have learnt this from their own experience of what God's grace could do with them—not many of them WISE AFTER THE WORLD'S FASHION, POWERFUL, OR WELL-BORN.

19 f. A very free rendering of Isa. 29.14 and 33.18, where the prophet sees in the disappearance of the Assyrian invader, despite all his administrative and military competence, a signal example of divine power.

23. Christ crucified

We shall realize better how this could be A STUMBLING-BLOCK TO THE JEWS if we translate as 'a crucified Messiah'

31. Another free rendering, this time of Jer. 9.23 f. and I Sam. 2.10 (LXX).

2.1. Mystery

Mysterion here means 'God's secret purpose'. The difference between this 'mystery' and those of the mystery religions is that their mysteries are reserved for the enlightenment of the few, the 'perfect', the initiates, while the mysteries of God are to be proclaimed, when the appropriate moment has arrived, to all the world. (Cf. Ignatius, *Ephesians* 19.1: 'There were three mysteries to be loudly proclaimed which were wrought in the silence of God: the virginity of Mary, her giving birth, and the death of the Lord. These were hidden from the prince of this world.')

7. A wisdom which we speak among the spiritually mature

What was this WISDOM OF GOD, this 'true wisdom' on which St Paul was so insistent? Plainly he had had more than enough of what the Corinthians understood by 'wisdom', for he contrives to repeat both the noun and the adjective so many times between 1.17 and 3.20 that his readers must have been heartily sorry they had ever used them. Speculation and 'philosophy', hair-splitting disputations, shallow rhetoric, intellectual conceit, all these things were involved in this WISDOM OF THIS WORLD. The key to the WISDOM OF GOD with which he confronts them is to be found in 1.24; 1.30; 2.7. If we study these verses and compare them with such a passage as 8.6, for example, FOR US THERE IS ONLY ONE GOD, THE FATHER, WHO IS THE ORIGIN OF ALL THINGS, AND THE END OF OUR BEING; ONLY ONE LORD, JESUS CHRIST, THE CREATOR OF ALL THINGS, WHO IS OUR WAY TO HIM, we find that what St Paul means by THE WISDOM OF GOD is really the whole divine plan of creation, redemption, and the consummation (or, as the thought sometimes runs, the restitution) of all things. In other words, divine wisdom is to be found in the gospel; through Jesus Christ this revelation has been given to the Church, where the divine Spirit dwells, interpreting to all who believe the secret thoughts of God himself (see 2.13, 16), far beyond the grasp of all the WISDOM OF THIS WORLD (2.6). This divine wisdom the Apostle sees as personified, incarnate, in Christ, a step in his thinking for which the personification of Wisdom in Prov. 8, Wisd. 7.22-7 and Ecclus. 24 had prepared the way. As such, Christ is the agent both of the creation of the world and of the new creation, redeemed mankind in the Church. This is the point in 8.6 of the description of Christ both as THE CREATOR OF ALL THINGS and as OUR WAY TO GOD. Similarly, in I Cor. 10.4, the description of Christ as the Rock in the wilderness, from whom comes the life-giving water, points forward to his saving work in the journeyings of the New Israel, through baptism and the Eucharist. The thought here outlined reached its full expression in Col. 1.16-20: IN HIM ALL CREATED THINGS TOOK THEIR BEING . . . HE TOO IS THAT HEAD WHOSE BODY IS THE CHURCH; IT BEGINS WITH HIM. . . . This is what the Apostles and the Church must reveal to all men; there is nothing reserved for special initiates. But the Corinthians have become so obsessed with themselves and their WISDOM that they cannot yet be described as SPIRITUALLY MATURE; as he tells them later (II Cor. 4.4) they are in danger of becoming like those unbelievers whose MINDS HAVE BEEN BLINDED BY THE GOD WHOM THIS WORLD WORSHIPS, so that the gospel light shines out for them in vain.

Among the perfect

The Greek word *teleios* is used for the 'initiates' in the mystery religion, but here its meaning is governed by the word *nēpios* (BABE) in 3.1. The *teleioi* are the SPIRITUALLY MATURE, those who reveal adult as opposed to childish characteristics. Men still relying on 'natural philosophy' of the kind that the Corinthians rated so highly cannot understand true wisdom unless they are prepared to forsake guidance of this kind and place themselves under the guidance of THE SPIRIT OF GOD (2.12).

8. The classic example of this blindness to the divine wisdom is the case of those who crucified Christ, which they could never have done had they not been so blinded. THE RULERS OF THIS WORLD here must surely be taken literally

of the actual rulers, secular and ecclesiastical, who were
responsible for the crucifixion. In Eph. 6.12 the responsibility for deeds of this kind is laid at the door of evil
spiritual powers, and it is part of the triumph of the resurrection that such powers are destroyed. But common as is
the thought of this SPIRITUAL WICKEDNESS IN HEAVENLY
PLACES in St Paul's mind, the context here calls for the
thought of the immediate human agents in the tragedy of
the crucifixion. W. L. Knox combines the two.[1] 'The
" rulers ", i.e. the angelic powers, . . . did not understand
God's purpose, which is known to every Christian, and
therefore crucified the Lord of glory. But this is simply
a transfer to the angelic rulers of the ignorance of the
rulers of the Jews in Acts 3.17. . . . It was a mere commonplace of contemporary thought that things on earth were
counterparts of things in heaven.' Such a line of thought
also had its value in keeping relationships both with the
Jewish and with the Roman authorities on a plane where
reconciliation was possible.

8-10. The Lord of Glory

Already in the Church there is a foretaste of that glory;
St Paul expresses it in one of his free renderings of a verse
from Isaiah, the prophet whom he quotes most frequently
(Isa. 64.4). The verses following are an expansion of what
this means; it is the power given to the Holy Spirit to enter
with Christ into the inner counsels of God himself.

13.. Read with RV margin INTERPRETING SPIRITUAL THINGS
TO SPIRITUAL MEN. These are the men who can be described
as SPIRITUALLY MATURE. The Corinthians revere men who
are *psychikoi*, not *pneumatikoi*, men who place all their
reliance on the intellect, who are lacking in all sense
of the supernatural, and move wholly on the natural
plane.

[1] *St Paul and the Church of the Gentiles*, 1939, Note IV, p. 221.

15 f. At first sight v. 15 seems likely to encourage the very spiritual pride which the Apostle is criticizing in the Corinthians; but what is NOT SUBJECT TO ANY MAN'S JUDGMENT is the wisdom imparted to him from on high, not any achievement of his own. It is the Spirit of God who GIVES LIGHT AND UNDERSTANDING TO THE SIMPLE (Ps. 119.130), who also gives to the new-born Christian new life in the Body of Christ. It is by virtue of the closeness of his union with Christ in his Body, the Church, that the Christian may be said to have THE MIND OF CHRIST and in virtue of this to JUDGE ALL THINGS (cf. 6.2 : YOU KNOW WELL ENOUGH THAT CHRISTIANS WILL JUDGE THE WORLD). In v. 16 St Paul moves directly from the thought of THE MIND OF THE LORD, that is, of Almighty God (Isa. 40.13) to THE MIND OF CHRIST seen as its equivalent.

THE CORINTHIANS' FACTIOUS SPIRIT REVEALS THEIR SPIRITUAL IMMATURITY

3.

This factious spirit confuses their view of the ministry and of the Church and is aggravated by their persistent dependence on THE WISDOM OF THIS WORLD.

3.1. as unto carnal
' As mere creatures of flesh and blood.'

3. carnal
The Greek word is slightly different; perhaps ' quite worldly in outlook' gives the meaning.

walk after the manner of men
'. . . and no different in your conduct from the ordinary run of men.'

5-9. The emphasis throughout is on God as the source of all ministry and all gifts, so that there may be anticipated in the Church that universal sovereignty which is described in 15.28, when GOD SHALL BE ALL IN ALL. We may see here, too, an emphasis on unity as necessary in the Church; the ministers may differ in both their talents and their tasks, but what they are concerned with is the work entrusted to them by the one God.

9. With this verse St Paul passes from the metaphor of husbandry to that of building.

10-15. The general sense of this passage reminds us of such parables as the Wheat and the Tares and the Dragnet. Despite the Church's foundation being truly laid in the saving life, death and resurrection of Christ, there is no guarantee that the building erected on it will be free from faults. The quality of the work varies, and will not become plain until it is tested in the fires of judgment. Even then, however mistaken his work may be, the man who has built on the one Foundation will be saved (v. 15), even though he may be as a BRAND PLUCKED FROM THE BURNING (Amos 4.11).

13. the day

As in I Thess. 5.4, we have here an echo of the Old Testament phrase THE DAY OF THE LORD, when all will be submitted to the final test and all worthless material will break down under the strain. Knox sees here a reference to purgatorial fire: 'We are to recognize that many whose actions in this world have had little value, will themselves escape condemnation, though only by passing through the fires of Purgatory.'[1] But this exegesis is not likely to be generally accepted. Cf. another Roman Catholic scholar,

[1] Knox, p. 359 n.

F. Prat, who writes:[1] 'The fire which the Apostle speaks of here is not the fire of purgatory, for this purifies but does not try, and has nothing to do with the work done.'

14. The thought of a reward for one's work is natural to humanity, and both our Lord and St Paul accept it; but the parable of the Labourers in the Vineyard, for example, and St Paul's conception of God's free grace, govern the meaning that we may attach to it. No one can claim to have merited a reward, for all must acknowledge themselves UNPROFITABLE SERVANTS.

16 f. The temple of God

This is the first time in St Paul's letters that we have put before us the conception of the Christian temple. It appears again from a different aspect in 6.19 f. Again, in II Cor. 5.1, we read that WE HAVE A BUILDING FROM GOD, A HOUSE NOT MADE WITH HANDS, ETERNAL, IN THE HEAVENS, and in II Cor. 6.16 we are described as A TEMPLE OF THE LIVING GOD. In Eph. 2.20-22 Christ is the CHIEF CORNER-STONE, IN WHOM EACH SEVERAL BUILDING, FITLY FRAMED TOGETHER, GROWETH INTO AN HOLY TEMPLE IN THE LORD; IN WHOM YE ALSO ARE BUILDED TOGETHER FOR AN HABITATION OF GOD THROUGH THE SPIRIT. We may also compare I Peter 2.4 f. (RSV): COME TO HIM, TO THAT LIVING STONE . . . AND LIKE LIVING STONES BE YOURSELVES BUILT INTO A SPIRITUAL HOUSE. (It is an interesting coincidence—does it indicate Peter's acquaintance with this epistle?—that I Peter 2 begins with the thought of the recipients of the letter as NEW-BORN BABES, who must LONG FOR THE PURE SPIRITUAL MILK, THAT BY IT THEY MAY GROW UP TO SALVATION.) We should note also John 1.14: THE WORD BECAME FLESH, AND MADE HIS TABERNACLE AMONG US; and John 2.19, 21: DESTROY THIS TEMPLE AND IN THREE DAYS I WILL RAISE IT UP AGAIN . . . BUT HE WAS SPEAKING ABOUT THE SANCTUARY OF HIS BODY.

[1] *The Theology of St Paul*, I, p. 96.

It is significant that v. 16 here begins with the words DON'T YOU KNOW or SURELY YOU KNOW, which suggests that the Corinthians can be assumed to be familiar with the rich complex of ideas and teaching that had already gathered around these two metaphors of Temple or Shrine and Body. Robinson (pp. 64 f.) rightly calls attention to the fact of the association of God or the Holy Spirit with the metaphor of building or temple, and notes that ' it is probably no accident that Paul does not use the phrase " the temple of Christ ".' On II Cor. 5.1, he points out (p. 76) that ' wherever Paul uses the word " building " (except in the purely figurative sense of " edification ") he means the Body of Christ, the Church.' We have already seen that St John (2.21) says that the Lord's body is the temple of God, and we may go on to note, for example, the idea of the superseding of the dead stones of the Temple of Judaism by the living stones of the New Israel, who, released by the Spirit from a localization of the worship of God at Jerusalem or on Mount Gerizim, worship him in Spirit and in truth with SPIRITUAL SACRIFICES. Or, again, we can see how Christians are taught that when Christ's body was raised from the tomb, they too were raised. ' For we, Christ's members, are included in that body, " made without hands ", which was nailed to the cross and raised " in three days " ' (Thornton, p. 319). When then we read in this letter of the temple of God, or the body, or the Body of Christ, we must always see these metaphors as related to one another and implying the doctrine of the risen Christ, living on in his Church as in a body, of which through the life-giving Spirit Christians are living parts, offering to God true and living worship, the New Israel inheriting the privileges and rendering the service which ISRAEL AFTER THE FLESH had rejected and refused.

In these verses St Paul has one particular object in view. He reminds the Corinthians that their factions and jealousies are a threat not just to themselves but to the Church of

God. Not only are they causing disunity; they are also profaning a sanctuary by their disputes. The word 'temple' in our English versions translates two Greek words, *naos* and *hieron*. Of these, the first stands for the inmost sanctuary, the Holy of Holies, and the second for the temple precincts in general. Here it is the first word that is used, and its use adds solemnity to the warning given. The Corinthian Christians are God's sanctuary, the dwelling-place of the Holy Spirit. Their quarrels and jealousies will ruin it, and their own ruin will follow (v. 17); the violation of holiness is fraught with danger.

18-23. St Paul returns to the explicit question of their tendency to set up one minister against another. The cause of it is their reliance upon human standards and judgment and their failure to see Paul or Apollos or Cephas or themselves, or indeed everything there is, in the setting of the divine plan, and this despite scriptural warnings (Job 5.13; Ps. 94.11) against shallow this-worldly views.

22 f. The thought here is similar to that in Rom. 8.38 f. The love of God in Christ is all-pervading and all-powerful, and those who belong to him, claiming nothing as their own (for all comes from God), yet see everything as given to them by God. All existing circumstances are in God's hands, and the MEMBERS OF CHRIST share in his universal sovereignty. At the same time, so long as they believe in him, nothing that can happen to them can separate them from his love. In a sense II Cor. 6.1-10 is an illustrative comment on the theme of these two verses.

Christ is God's
   i.e. in the sense of I Cor. 15.28. The work of Christ is part of the divine plan and cannot be thought of apart from it. (See note there.)

THE APOSTOLIC TASK AND RESPONSIBILITY
RE-STATED

4.

4.1-5. St Paul finds it necessary to re-state his apostolic functions and to make plain to whom he is responsible for the way in which he discharges them. He is A STEWARD OF THE MYSTERIES OF GOD (4.1). He has used this word MYSTERY already, and it is he who uses it most frequently in the New Testament. By it he means not a secret to be revealed to a few chosen initiates, but God's plan as it has lain hidden in the divine foreknowledge until the time has come for it to be revealed to those whom he has chosen, and through them to all mankind. When this plan is thought of in all its grandeur, then the MYSTERY to be revealed is the staggering truth, to be universally proclaimed, of the universality of the gospel; God's plan is for the salvation of all (see Rom. 16.25-7; it is in the same sense as there, no doubt, that the word 'mystery' is used in ch. 2 of this epistle). But it is also used of parts of the whole divine scheme of salvation; and it is in this partial sense that is used in 15.51; BEHOLD I SHOW YOU A MYSTERY—God's plan to overcome death.

1. Ministers . . . and stewards
The Corinthians had forgotten that those who had brought them the gospel were following the example of their Master who had said: I AM AMONG YOU AS HE THAT SERVETH. St Paul reminds them that he and his fellow-workers are servants of God and of the Church bringing to them NO OTHER GOSPEL than that entrusted to them by God, to whom they are responsible, as major-domos over the household of God.

3. that I should be judged

Rather: ' be put on my trial '.

man's judgment

Literally ' man's day '. St Paul, with the Judgment Day of God in mind (2.13 above), uses the phrase to describe a human tribunal. (ICC refers to Job 9.33: THERE IS NO DAYS-MAN BETWEEN US, meaning an arbiter or umpire.)

4. If others know too little about him to enable them to form a judgment, the same is true of his own judgment of himself.

I know nothing by myself (AV)

Better ' I KNOW NOTHING AGAINST MYSELF ', for ' by ' here is an archaism equivalent to ' against '. But despite his own conviction that his conscience is clear, he, like others, does not know himself well enough to give a verdict of acquittal.

5. Only God knows all the facts and circumstances, and only when *his* judgments are pronounced shall we know who is innocent and who is guilty, for THE LORD SEETH NOT AS A MAN SEETH, FOR MAN LOOKETH UPON THE OUTWARD APPEARANCE, BUT THE LORD LOOKETH UPON THE HEART (I Sam. 16.7).

6. St Paul goes on to say, in a verse of considerable obscurity, that the references he has been making to Apollos and himself have been made deliberately in order to show the Corinthians that the absence of rivalry between them, in the exercise of the gifts God has given them, should be the example they ought to follow. No satisfactory meaning has been suggested for the phrase NOT TO GO BEYOND WHAT HAS BEEN WRITTEN. Phillips translates it as NOT TO ASSESS A MAN ABOVE HIS VALUE IN GOD'S SIGHT. It may be some proverbial expression to which we no longer have the clue.

7 f. The dominant thought is no doubt that no man ought to boast of his gifts or station, because all things come from God. But WITHOUT ANY HELP FROM US suggests by its ironical tone that the Corinthians are behaving as if they were far in advance of their teachers, and as if the various gifts which they are manifesting are entirely due to themselves. They consider themselves leaders in things spiritual, but apostolic experience of what leadership in the Church of God means is very different.

In these verses the root sin of the Corinthian Church, spiritual pride, is brought out into the open, and the Apostle ironically contrasts their feeling of superiority and self-satisfaction with the life of an Apostle, one of constant shame and humiliation, of suffering and slander, and all for Christ's sake (4.9-13). But he is far from despairing of them, and hopes with fatherly love to visit them and recall them to the following of the Christian way which he taught them.

15. *Paidagōgos* was not what we understand by 'pedagogue'; he might be a teacher, but as he was almost without exception a slave this was not often the case. Generally he was the equivalent of a nursemaid whose duty it was to take care of children on their walks and on their way to school, and to bring them safely home. Here the best translation would probably be 'supervisor' or 'guardian'. In Gal. 3.24, the emphasis is rather on actual teaching, and the word should be translated 'tutor'.

17. The evidence, such as it is, seems to suggest that this visit by Timothy never took place. The purpose of sending him was that his loyalty and humility should bring back to the memory of the Corinthians the life, example and teaching of the one who had brought them the gospel, and was therefore their true 'father-in-God', but whom some of them seemed now to have forgotten.

18. some are puffed up

The Greek verb, derived from the same root as the noun *phusa*, 'a pair of bellows', is repeated twice in a few sentences (see 5.2), and evidently strikes St Paul as particularly apt to describe the windy complacency that some of his converts had developed.

20. kingdom of God

See note on 6.10. Here the meaning is related to such a saying of our Lord's as THE KINGDOM OF GOD IS WITHIN YOU. It is the inward reality which permeates and gives meaning to the external reality of the Christian Church, the community where God's writ runs, through the indwelling of the Spirit.

A BAD CASE OF IMMORALITY

5.

Low moral standards, particularly in sexual matters, complicated the spread of the gospel in the Gentile world, and occupied the attention of Christian leaders brought up under the moral discipline of the Mosaic Law; hence the warning against sexual licence in Acts 15.29. Such complications would be especially to the fore in Corinth, where moral standards were notoriously low; immorality had the backing of religious practice, and there was a tendency to say that 'spiritual' people could regard bodily sin as a matter completely indifferent. The Corinthians, though more excitable and unstable than the Thessalonians, were not unique in their failings. In I Thess. 4.3 f., for example, St Paul finds it necessary to write to them, WHAT GOD ASKS OF YOU IS THAT YOU SHOULD SANCTIFY YOURSELVES AND KEEP YOURSELVES CLEAR OF FORNICATION. EACH OF YOU MUST LEARN TO CONTROL HIS OWN BODY . . . NOT YIELDING TO THE PROMPTINGS OF PASSION AS THE HEATHEN DO. St Paul finds himself obliged to act sternly, for a case of incest has been reported to him which, for one reason or another, the Corinthian Christians seem to have tolerated, at least in the sense that they took no positive action against the sinners. We have no exact details of the case, but it was plainly flagrant. Far from grieving over it, however, Corinthian spiritual pride has survived it all; they are still PUFFED UP (v.2).

5. But St Paul, though far from the scene of the sin, has been deeply moved, and has passed sentence on the sinner; he is to be expelled from the Christian community, where God's reign is accepted, and left once more to that non-Christian world where evil is supreme; they are to DELIVER SUCH A ONE UNTO SATAN. Then he may learn, St Paul seems to think by actual physical suffering, the deadly nature of the sins of the flesh, and also realize that if he is to be amongst ' the saved ' he will have to MORTIFY THE DEEDS OF THE BODY. All this seems to be implicit in the words FOR THE DESTRUCTION OF THE FLESH.

In this verse we have the beginnings of ecclesiastical discipline; it is a solemn act of excommunication, initiated by the Apostle and to be carried out by the Christian community UNDER THE AUTHORITY OF THE LORD JESUS, for it is this sovereign authority that is invoked for this solemn purpose, as much as for the working of miracles or for exorcism, when the ' Name ' of Jesus is solemnly invoked (cf. Acts 4.7; 19.13). The purpose of this solemn excommunication was not only punitive, but remedial and in the hope that, repentant, the sinner might be restored to the community (cf. II Cor. 2.6, 10; and I Tim. 1.20, where Hymenaeus and Alexander are DELIVERED TO SATAN, THAT THEY MAY BE TAUGHT NOT TO BLASPHEME).

6-8. These verses give us an indication of some of the teaching that must have been given to the Corinthian Church. We shall not be mistaken if we see constant references to a ' corpus ' of teaching, given to the infant church, throughout this epistle. Not only are there the assumptions that the main lines of thought and doctrine on such subjects as baptism, the Eucharist, the Body of Christ, the resurrection, are familiar to those to whom it is written. There is also, no fewer that five times in this chapter alone, the appearance of a formula presupposing previous instruction which may be translated as SURELY YOU KNOW or

DON'T YOU REMEMBER? or YOU KNOW WELL ENOUGH.

7. Cleanse out the old leaven

It may well be that St Paul was writing at or near the passover (see 16.8: TILL PENTECOST I SHALL BE STAYING AT EPHESUS), or he may simply be proclaiming that the joy of Easter had made all life a passover feast for Christians; but at all events, these Christians had been taught to see the passover, of the Jews as a 'type' fulfilled in Christ, the true passover, to whom they had been called. Now they are reminded of the symbolism of those scrupulous Jewish searches, in preparation for the passover, for even the smallest crumb of leavened bread. They are Christians; for them the true Paschal Lamb has been slain; their whole life ought to be a passover, and in preparation for it every trace of evil should be removed.

9-13. St Paul turns aside to deal in a parenthesis with what might be described as 'evasive action' by the Corinthian Christians. Concealing from him the real situation, they had asked him whether he had really meant, in an earlier letter, that they were TO HAVE NOTHING TO DO WITH MEN OF EVIL LIFE. How was this practicable, they asked, in the kind of world they lived in? The Apostle replies that he was not thinking of sinners outside the Church, but of those within; and he repeats his summons to excommunication in such cases.

IV

LAWSUITS BEFORE HEATHEN COURTS

6.

THESE ARE QUITE INCONSISTENT WITH CHRISTIAN BEHAVIOUR

6.1-11

It may be that here, too, St Paul puts before us the beginning of another form of Christian discipline—ecclesiastical courts. Jews living in heathen countries were accustomed to settle their own disputes in their own courts, and no doubt St Paul expected his converts to follow such an admirable precedent. We must not think of him as condemning Roman courts of law, however; he knew from his own experience their impartiality in the administration of justice, and in Rom. 13 he makes it quite plain that Christians must obey them as divinely appointed guardians of law and order. But disputes such as the Corinthian Christians had become involved in were not matters that should be dragged out into the publicity of the courts; they should be settled among themselves according to their own standards of justice. (Note again similar troubles at Thessalonica; NONE OF YOU IS TO BE EXORBITANT OR TO TAKE ADVANTAGE OF HIS BROTHER IN HIS BUSINESS DEALINGS: I Thess. 4.6.)

1. the saints

The word translated 'saints' really means no more than

81

'Christians', and this is probably the best translation of it, provided that we remember that by this word St Paul would understand 'persons consecrated to God, professing Christ and sanctified by the Spirit'.[1]

2 f. Once again the Apostle is able to appeal to his readers' familiarity with the common Christian teaching of the certainty of the Messianic Age, when the authority of the Messiah and his faithful followers would be universal and universally acknowledged, even beyond the confines of this world. He uses this teaching to mark vividly the contrast between the majesty of their calling and the pettiness of the Corinthian practice, and to emphasize the earth-bound nature of their preoccupations.

4. A difficult verse, but it may carry a sarcastic reference to the spiritual pride with which the Corinthians were obsessed, and the feeling of superiority over the unenlightened which they enjoyed. If so, we may translate: DO YOU, THEN, IF YOU HAVE BUSINESS QUARRELS, HAVE RESORT TO THOSE WHOM YOU, AS CHRISTIANS, THINK NOTHING OF? SHAME ON YOU! SURELY YOU CAN FIND ONE OF YOURSELVES WISE ENOUGH TO JUDGE BETWEEN YOU. This seems to make a somewhat strained sense, however, and it would be better to drop the question-mark at the end of v. 4 and make it a sarcastic imperative: 'If you must have disputes about these very ordinary matters that seem to worry you so much, then let your most ordinary members settle them. But it is a shame that I have to write to you like this! Surely you must have amongst you at any rate *one* Christian wise enough to settle these fraternal disputes, and so make it unnecessary to take your quarrels off to the law-courts of the heathen.'

5-11. The fact is that despite their baptism and all the

[1] O. S. Rankin, *TWBB*, art. 'Saints'.

privileges it brought with it (v. 11), the Corinthians are far from understanding even the elementary teaching of the gospel about the right attitude of the Christian to those who do him wrong. (Perhaps we have a glance in v. 7 at such teaching as Matt. 5.40: IF ANYONE WANTS TO SUE YOU AND TAKE YOUR COAT, MAKE HIM A PRESENT OF YOUR CLOAK AS WELL.) They have not even grasped the deadly nature of sins such as fornication, sodomy, adultery or theft.

10. the kingdom of God

Here the Apostle is thinking of 'that Messianic kingdom which is the reward and goal in heaven of the Christian life here below'.[1] Elsewhere, as in 4.20, he is thinking of that acceptance of the will of God, whether by individuals or communities, which means their 'entrance into the kingdom' or their 'entrance into life'. As with ETERNAL LIFE in the Fourth Gospel, we can begin to enjoy here the blessings of the kingdom, but human sin and other hindrances delay its consummation till hereafter.

WHY FORNICATION IS SUCH A SERIOUS MATTER

6.12-20

12-20. The catalogue of vices in v. 10 brings to St Paul's mind both the question of fornication and the Corinthian attitude towards it. Once again the Corinthians have revealed an elementary failure to realize the implications of their baptism, by which they had been made MEMBERS OF CHRIST and had received the indwelling of the Holy Spirit. Moreover, as if this were not enough, the meaning of the death of Christ has escaped them, too; he who had made

[1] Alan Richardson, *TWBB*, art. 'Kingdom of God'.

them his at baptism seals what he has done by his death, which rescues them from their slavery to sin and evil.

12. All things are possible to me

Possibly a Corinthian catch-phrase to express the complete freedom which Christianity bestows. St Paul does not deny it, but points out that liberty for a Christian is limited by the effect of his actions on others. He cannot live as if he were alone in the world. Moreover, his actions have an influence not only over others but on himself; if he has found that a certain line of action has meant 'occasions of sin', it must be abandoned, or he may no longer be master of himself, and therefore no longer free, but controlled by this desire or that.

13. Probably a proverbial expression, extended by the Corinthians to cover the satisfaction of all bodily appetites as 'natural'. Sexual desires, like the desire for food, are 'natural' and ought to be satisfied.

The word *koilia*, 'belly', here stands for the same thing as St Paul's word 'flesh': it is that part of human nature which is essentially connected with this transient temporal order and finds its satisfaction in material things. To think of the future life in terms merely of a continuation of the present, and that sometimes in a crudely materialistic manner, was the error of some Pharisees, and led to such stock attacks on them by the Sadducees as are recorded in Mark 12.18-27 (the question about the woman who was married seven times). Such views were contemptuously rejected by our Lord, and this teaching finds an echo here; see also 15.50. Our one word 'body' translates the two Greek words *sarx* and *sōma*; both represent the whole man looked at from different angles. Robinson (p. 34 n.) quotes an illuminating comment on this passage by Professor P. Althaus: 'The body is, on the one hand, wholly *koilia*, that is, the sum of the sensual functions which make our earthly life possible; as such it passes away with this earthly world. On the other hand, the body is wholly *sōma*, that is, the carrier and object of our action, expression and form; as such it is a limb of the body of the risen Christ and will be raised with the personality.'

the body is . . . for the Lord, and the Lord for the body

The true understanding of the body and its nature is grasped when we realize that we are here to serve the Lord, and that the indispensable part the body has to play in this service is made plain to us by the Incarnation, and by the Lord's use of the body in that divine act. Moreover, the proverb just quoted is concerned with physical existence and therefore with this life; the body is destined to be transformed; it has an eternal significance. This it derives from baptism and Christ's redeeming work; it is a vital part of the whole redeemed personality. Indeed, from the Hebrew point of view, the body is our self, expressing itself. Fornication is a denial of all this is a special way, for ' fornication, like marriage, brings a man and a woman into a relation so close and powerful that there may almost be said to be a mingling of personality' (Goudge, p. 50). If we think of the Christian, made by baptism a living part of the Body of Christ, the Church, and then see the Church as the Bride of Christ—a metaphor used in this very correspondence (see II Cor. 11.2: I ESPOUSED YOU TO ONE HUSBAND) and fully worked out in Eph. 5.22 f.—we see something of the horror with which St Paul regarded fornication. It is spiritual adultery. The Apostle seems to suggest that once a man's body has been used for fornication, it is no longer his to offer to God. We may not be able to follow him in the most rigorist interpretation of this line of thought, but we are hardly likely to find a more ' positive ' approach to the sins of the flesh than that put before us here. Baptism, the gift of the Spirit, the atonement, the resurrection, all these are brought to bear upon OUR BODIES.

We cannot do what we please with what we have handed over to God to become a holy sanctuary, to be his possession for eternity. There is a relationship between our bodies and our whole personal existence, an existence not only in time but in eternity. Hence the Apostle's emphasis on the resurrection of the body, the personality, as against the wholly 'earthy' FLESH AND BLOOD (ch. 15).

18. This difficult verse is probably best understood, as ICC suggests, by a reference to our Lord's words about the SIN AGAINST THE HOLY GHOST (Matt. 12.31). We are to think of other sins as grievous indeed, but not involving, as this one of fornication does, an act of sacrilege, a setting up, in the shrine of the Holy Ghost, of the evil spirit of lust; for there can be no doubt that St Paul's thinking about fornication was profoundly affected by the fact that the same word *porneia* was used by the Jews for fornication and idolatry. It is a sin which of itself involves a profanation of the whole redeemed and spirit-dwelt personality. In 3.16 f. St Paul has already compared the whole Christian Church to a sanctuary of God the Holy Spirit, and warned the Corinthians that their factions and quarrels are not only a breach of unity but an act of sacrilege, a profanation of the holy. Here in this verse we have 'the particularization of the general statement about the Church as the temple of God already enunciated in ch. 3'.[1] See, for the general line of thought, Rom. 12.1: I APPEAL TO YOU, THEREFORE, BRETHREN . . . TO PRESENT YOUR BODIES AS A LIVING SACRIFICE, HOLY, ACCEPTABLE TO GOD, WHICH IS YOUR SPIRITUAL WORSHIP, and I Peter 2.5.

[1] Selwyn, *I Peter*, Note H, p. 289.

V

A QUESTION FROM THE CORIN-THIANS: MARRIAGE PROBLEMS

7.

St Paul now turns from what he has heard to particular problems on which the Corinthian Church has consulted him. We note throughout how marked is his sense of his apostolic authority, and, at this stage of his dealings with this church, that there is no suggestion that anyone is going to question it. But we notice, too, how scrupulously careful he is to distinguish between his own rulings and any commands, precepts or sayings that can be traced directly to the Lord Jesus himself. It used to be the fashion amongst New Testament scholars—and the influence of it is still with us—to write as if St Paul had transformed the 'simple gospel' received from Jesus into an elaborate doctrinal system, borrowing heavily from paganism, and particularly from the mystery religions. It is difficult to see how anyone could have made this assumption, when we note in vv. 10 and 25 of this chapter the care which St Paul exercises in distinguishing between what we might call dominical and Pauline directions, and when we remember, too, the solemn references to the common traditions of the Church with which he introduces the subject of the Eucharist (ch. 11) and the resurrection (ch. 15). We may note Moffatt's balanced conclusion (p. 80): 'If anyone in the primitive Church had creative literary genius, it was Paul. It is historically of high importance that he did not feel at liberty to create a saying of Jesus, even when, as here, it would have been highly convenient in order to settle a disputed point of Christian behaviour.'

Consequently the beginnings of Christian casuistry which we have in this epistle set the standard for this necessary duty of the Christian Church throughout the centuries. The word ' casuistry ' has gathered round itself a dubious atmosphere, but in its true sense of the application of moral principles to special cases it is indispensable in the daily life and pastoral work of the Christian, and particularly of the Christian pastor. This chapter, where one of the first and greatest of her pastors finds himself faced with the pressing and practical problems of his flock, sets a standard and provides directions which are a model for all his successors. And in no human relationships is such application of principles to practice and experience more urgent and necessary than in the relations between the sexes and particularly in marriage.

1-9. Here there are two problems on which the Apostle has been consulted; in the case of married people ought sexual relations to be abandoned, and in the case of those who are not married, ought they to aim at the celibate life, and not marry at all? No doubt these questions were prompted by scruples of diverse kinds. There were those who under the influence of some contemporary religious ideas regarded the body and its functions as in themselves evil; there were others (and they would have been supported not only in pagan but in Jewish thought) who felt that intercourse in marriage might be a great hindrance to spiritual progress; there were others, again, who were convinced of the imminence of the Second Coming and felt that anything which interfered with their preparation for this must be surrendered.

3-6. St Paul's answers are clear and are dictated by healthy moral thinking and practical commonsense. Sex-experience has its rightful place in marriage and if it is to be put on one side for a time, even for spiritual reasons, it must be with the willing consent of both parties; this they owe to one another. Any one-sided withdrawal in an undisciplined place such as Corinth may well lead to sin.

He will have nothing to do with Corinthian extremes, an example of which he is probably quoting in v. 1.

7-9. In these verses we have perhaps his greatest contribution to the subject, the full implications of which have probably not even yet been appreciated by the Church at large. For his own part he thinks detachment from all earthly ties is best, but it is a question of vocation and of the gifts bestowed by God. Marriage and celibacy are two vocations; what matters is that we should all be loyal to God's calling, different as it may be for each of us. We see this thought expanded later in this epistle (ch. 11) and it may well be that St Paul has in mind our Lord's words on this very subject of dedicated celibacy (Matt. 19.11 f.), and how it is, for some, a precept which they *must* obey. It is sometimes argued that St Paul is here taking a low view of marriage, (the same difficulty is sometimes felt about the Prayer Book's attitude as set out, for example, in the Preface of the 1662 Marriage Service), but we must remember that he is answering questions from people who had to face the question of marriage as it might help them to lead a life of chastity in a city where all the pressure was the other way. We may look at Eph. 5 to see what he wrote when he was picturing Christian marriage at its true level.

10 f. The third Corinthian question concerned the possibility of divorce. Here St Paul takes his stand on Christ's own teaching (Mark 10.9; Luke 16.18). He forbids divorce absolutely and it is interesting that there is here no reference to the 'Matthaean exception' (Matt. 5.32). Indeed it is a striking fact that this Matthaean passage is nowhere echoed in the marriage teaching of the Church until after Justinian, and, like St Paul, we may take it as a fact that Christ forbade remarriage in the lifetime of the partner to one's marriage. We may catch a sidelight perhaps on women's influence in Corinthian Christianity in the fact that St Paul deals first with the wife wishing to divorce her husband; and he may indeed have a particular case in mind.

12-16. The fourth question now follows: what about a marriage in which one partner is converted to Christianity while the other remains heathen? This, in the nature of things, is not dealt with in any saying of Christ's, and St Paul has to give guidance on it in virtue of his own apostolic authority (v. 12). What he says takes cognisance of the fact that in a 'mixed marriage' of this kind there may well be severe tensions and strains; differing standards of morality can cause much difficulty. This is not the life that God means Christians to lead (v. 15: GOD HAS CALLED US TO LIVE IN PEACE). The first step to separation must not come from the Christian partner; the initiative must come from the other side. In any case St Paul does not contemplate remarriage (v. 11 and cf. v. 39).

14. We have here the other aspect of St Paul's view of the effect of sexual intercourse as involving the whole personality; in the case of fornication there is corruption of the Christian; in this case there is a 'consecration' of the non-Christian.

Otherwise your children would be unholy instead of being consecrated to God (Moffatt).

This is probably a reference to Jewish practice, where ' when heathen came over into Judaism their children also were subjected along with them to proselyte baptism. On the other hand, such children as were born only after the conversion of their parents did not have to be baptized. They ranked as sanctified through their parents.'[1]

17-24. Possibly with v. 7 in mind the Apostle concludes his advice on these particular marriage problems with a general principle of far-reaching effect. IN EACH CASE LET PEOPLE BE CONTENT WITH THE LOT WHICH GOD HAS ASSIGNED THEM, AND WITH THE CONDITION IN WHICH GOD'S CALL HAS COME TO THEM, AND LET THEM CONTINUE IN THAT COURSE SO FAR AS MAY BE. THIS IS THE RULE I AM LAYING DOWN FOR ALL THE CHURCHES.[2]

He then illustrates this principle as it would apply in different walks in life, but in a quite general way. We shall be as mistaken if we try to derive specific teaching from the illustrations (e.g., as to the Apostle's view of slavery) as we would in pressing the details of one of our Lord's parables.

25-40. These verses deal with another question from the Corinthians. But we have first to decide what it was (25 and 36-38). (a) Some think that we have here a very early example of pseudo-ascetic practice, denounced as early as St Cyprian and forbidden by the Council of Nicaea, whereby clerics had unmarried women to live with them as 'spiritual sisters', with resultant scandals when, as Gibbon remarked, 'Insulted Nature sometimes claimed her revenge.' If this is the case here, St Paul is faced with people who have ventured on this experiment and are finding 'Nature' becoming too much for them. This interpretation is favoured by Ephraim the Syrian (fourth century), but he may well have been reading back into this passage practices of his own times. (b) Another possibility is that

[1] Cullmann, *Baptism in the New Testament* (Studies in Biblical Theology 1), 1950, p. 25.
[2] ICC, p. 137.

the passage refers to a man's own unmarried daughters; if
so we have another example of difficulties brought about
by the prevailing expectation of a speedy Second Coming.
Obviously, from such verses as 26 and still more 29-31,
this thought is very much to the fore. If this is true, then,
remembering that a daughter had no say in such a matter,
we have here the problem of anxious heads of families
wondering where their duty lay. Was it wise, in view of the
End, or of its attendant troubles, to allow their daughters
to enter upon marriage at all? (In Thessalonica this anxiety
took the form of neglect of business and general reckless-
ness about their affairs: I Thess. 4.11.) (c) A third
explanation is that we have here a reference to a husband
betrothed but not yet married. (This is the view of RSV,
which translates VIRGIN as BETROTHED.) (d) Somewhat akin
to this is the suggestion that the problem is one of people
who have married but have refrained from consummating
the marriage, perhaps by mutual consent in the circumstances that St Paul has already described earlier in the
chapter (v. 5). Certainty does not seem possible, but on the
whole (b), accepted by Goudge and by the ICC, appears
the most likely, especially if we may detect here an echo of
the apocalyptic passage incorporated in Luke 17.20-37, and
particularly v. 27: THEY ATE, THEY DRANK, THEY MARRIED,
THEY WERE GIVEN IN MARRIAGE; UNTIL THE DAY CAME WHEN
. . . THE FLOOD DESTROYED THEM ALL. SO SHALL IT BE IN
THE DAYS OF THE SON OF MAN. Observe in vv. 25 and 40
the Apostle's care in explaining that he is here neither
quoting the Lord Jesus nor giving an apostolic ruling, but
simply giving his own considered opinion; in v. 40 he adds
half-ironically, AND I SUPPOSE I HAVE THE SPIRIT OF GOD
AS WELL AS OTHER PEOPLE (Moffatt).

25-36. After raising the question sent him with the words
NOW CONCERNING VIRGINS etc., St Paul digresses to make
again, with a different emphasis, the point he had made

just before, that every Christian should strive to serve God in the particular state or calling he is in. But IN THE IM-MINENT DISTRESS OF THESE DAYS marriage and family life will bring special problems with them, and though there is no question of its being wrong for Christians to marry, even in times like these, they must remember what will be involved. To put it briefly, with the Second Coming only just round the corner. Christians must practise detachment and not become immersed in anything or anybody.

35. not that I may cast a snare upon you (AV, RV).

Better NOT THAT I WANT TO RESTRICT YOUR FREEDOM (Moffatt). The word *brochos* means a noose, rather than a 'snare', and the Apostle means that what he is saying is intended to help them so to arrange their lives as to promote decorum and to enable them to serve the Lord whole-heartedly, without let or hindrance.

39 f. This return to the question of the remarriage of widows (already touched on in v. 8) may be due to some special problems in connection with them at Corinth. In ancient society widowhood must have been economically a most precarious state and more than once in the New Testament we find the Christian Church concerned with the problem presented by it.

The subject is treated fully in I Tim. 5: evidently in return for relief and maintenance widows were expected to devote themselves to prayer and good works; they also had to fulfil certain conditions before they could be recognized as deserving support from the Church. They seem indeed to have been formally 'enrolled' and to have constituted a distinct group within the Church.

Some rigorist ascetics were opposed to their marrying again, but St Paul will have none of this. Re-asserting (39) his prohibition of marriage in the lifetime of a partner to a marriage that had broken up, he goes on to say that upon the death of that partner one is free to marry as one pleases except that it should be with a Christian.

The chapter has found many severe critics (see for example the notes in Moffatt, especially p. 96) of St Paul's teaching on marriage and celibacy. But it must be seen in its context (the sense of the imminence of the End, the immoral surroundings of Corinth and the prevalent low views of marriage). It must be seen, too, in the light of the teaching on marriage in Eph. 5, where 'marriage is honoured by reason of its integration into the Body of Christ. Marriage and family in the course of the time between the resurrection and the Parousia of Jesus have no kind of inherent value. But by reason of their integration into the Church they do indeed possess a value which does not belong to them in themselves. I Cor. 7 does not represent a fundamentally different position from Eph. 5.22 ff.'[1] Celibacy and marriage are both set before us by St Paul as vocations to which we may be called. In the exceptional conditions under which he believed himself to be writing he regards the celibate life as best fitted to the service of God. He never suggests that marriage, if such be a Christian's vocation, excludes him or her from the highest blessings of the Christian life. But the need for the witness of the celibate life, deliberately accepted and deliberately renunciatory, is constant in the life of the Church, which must always be in a sense eschatological, filled with urgency, for THE TIME IS SHORT.

[1] Cullmann, *Baptism in the New Testament*, p. 43 and p. 45 n.

VI

THINGS SACRIFICED TO IDOLS

8.–11.1

THOSE WHO REALIZE THAT IDOLS ARE NON-ENTITIES MUST NOT USE THEIR KNOWLEDGE IN A WAY THAT WOULD HINDER OTHERS

8.

This was evidently, with marriage, a major problem for Christians at Corinth, and St Paul deals with it at some length. At first sight it seems to many modern Christians remote from anything in their experience and curiously unreal, one of those things which seem to mark biblical times and people off from our own age by an almost impassable gulf. But once we realize the extent to which the subject was bound up with daily life in Corinth, it takes on a somewhat different appearance. Even the meat sold in butchers' shops would nearly always have been killed in a temple and therefore dedicated to some god or other; some was burned on the altar; some was eaten on the temple premises at one of the regular feasts of the numerous guilds and societies, or at some more elaborate banquet in honour of the god (cf. 10.20 f.); and the surplus was then bought up by the butchers for public sale; so that even at meals in private houses the meat eaten would be IDOL-MEAT. In fact social life of any kind, whether in high society or low, could hardly be lived by Christians in Corinth without this

problem of what to do about 'idol-meats' arising. When
we realize this, this apparently irrelevant chapter is seen
at once to be concerned with problems which are contemporary for many of us. It is, or ought to be, impossible for
us to isolate ourselves from the missionary work of the
Church, and in the overseas mission field similar problems
are urgent. In view of the sexual practices associated with
many tribal initiation rites, for example, to what extent, if
any, ought African Christians to have anything to do with
them? African dances, again, are very much bound up with
African social life and are almost always performed
with the idea in the background of an African deity to be
charmed or propitiated. Indian marriage customs are
another case in point, attendance at which is regarded by
the Christian Church in Travancore as so compromising as
to require suspension from church membership for the
offender.[1] Is the Christian convert to cut himself off from
such occasions, and if so, what kind of a life is he expected
to lead? Amongst ourselves there may be occasions when
as Christians we feel bound to give up some practice or
custom in itself harmless enough, because of its implications
or because of the harm it does to others. In the matter of in-
toxicating drinks, for example, there are some Christians who
feel total abstinence is the only way for a Christian; others
are content with temperance; others are hardly aware of
any problem at all. Christians who have scruples about this
or that in the society in which they live are a persistent
phenomenon, and what St Paul had to say to Corinthian
Christians thus perplexed is still very much to the point.
The guiding principle must be twofold: all must be done
for God, and all we do must help and not hinder our fellow-
Christians.

1-6. Some of the Corinthians claimed to have received

[1] Sydney Cave, *The Gospel of St Paul*, 1928, p. 147, quoted by
Moffatt, p. 114.

special spiritual enlightenment, and therefore to see clearly that idols had no existence, and that therefore Christians could eat of what had been offered to idols without any scruple, for the performance had been devoid of any meaning and could have no effect whatever. St Paul agrees (though 10.19-21 shows that he has reservations), but vv. 7-13 goes on to show that the matter is not so simply disposed of.

1. we all have knowledge

Probably a Corinthian catch phrase: difficult to translate, for it is a claim to far more than we understand by 'knowledge'. The Apostle goes on to point out that whatever it is, it is liable to lead to pride and spiritual blindness, and that universal love rather than universal knowledge is what is needed, for it is unselfishly constructive and not self-centred.

6. one Lord Jesus . . . we through him

Our Lord is put before us as the agent both of our Creation and of our Redemption. Compare John 1.3, EVERY-THING CAME INTO BEING BY HIM, and Heb. 1.2, GOD HAS SPOKEN TO US BY HIS SON . . . BY WHOM HE MADE THE WORLDS. Moffatt points out (p. 109) that in this verse we are confronted with a confession of faith. As in I Tim. 3.16 we are shown 'how the initial forms of the creed were intended to be sung or chanted, as spontaneous outbursts of of heart and mind'.

7-13. The thought behind these verses might well be the saying of Jesus in Matt. 18.6, IF ANYONE HURTS THE CONSCIENCE OF ONE OF THESE LITTLE ONES THAT BELIEVE IN ME, HE HAD BETTER HAVE BEEN DROWNED IN THE DEPTHS OF THE SEA. The point is that at Corinth there may well be Christians, of no great mental gifts or particularly strong wills, who after a struggle have come to feel that it is wrong

G

for them as Christians to share in these IDOL-MEATS. Then,
seeing their fellow-Christians who HAVE KNOWLEDGE partaking of them, they follow suit, despite the arguments
of their conscience, with consequent wretchedness and sin.
And this tragedy is brought about through the simple in-
ability of some Christians to see that what matters is the
love of the brethren and our attitude to them. Christ died
for them, and it is by our attitude to them that we shall be
judged. Whether we are 'liberal' or 'scrupulous' in our
attitude to the question at issue is of no importance along-
side this.

7. their conscience

Syneidesis, originally a word meaning 'co-knowledge' or
'consciousness', came to be used in a way corresponding to
our modern use of the word conscience, but somewhat more
narrowly—in the sense that it tends to be used rather of
judgment given upon actions already past than in the sense
of a general guide for conduct both private and public.
This latter sense is, however, also to be found, as in this
verse and v. 10. In The Vocabulary of the Greek New
Testament (Moulton and Milligan) an amusing example
of the transition from one meaning to another is given from
the papyri where a woman is reported as being 'oppressed
by the consciousness of what she had appropriated both of
the furniture and articles in store'.

A DIGRESSION: AN APPEAL TO THE
APOSTLE'S OWN PRACTICE

9.

St Paul turns aside from the direct treatment of the question he has been asked, to illustrate from his own practice
the advice he has given to the Corinthians. Briefly, it was

that whatever their own gifts might be, there would be times when, in the service of God, they would have to be surrendered or left in abeyance in consideration of the needs of others. Incidentally, he may have in mind some criticism of his status or line of conduct as an Apostle (later on, by the time II Corinthians was written, this had become a pressing question), but if so, it does not seem to have been serious and certainly was not the primary object of this section of the letter.

1. He shares with the Corinthians the 'freedom' of a Christian, but in addition he enjoys the authority of an Apostle, guaranteed by his vision of JESUS OUR LORD and by the apostolic work he had done in the preaching of the gospel at Corinth and in the founding of the church there.

4-18. As an Apostle he has certain unquestionable rights; he has the right to maintenance, for example, both for himself and for his wife, if like others he were married. He has full scriptural support for this right of maintenance, if he cared to claim it (vv. 9 and 13), as well as the support of commonsense (v. 7). But he has deliberately refused all such maintenance; he does not criticize others who accept it, as they have a perfect right to do; but so far as he personally is concerned he has decided that he will not exercise his rights; he has determined that his preaching of the gospel will thus be best served.

5. a sister, a wife (AV)

The Greek words for both 'brother' and 'sister' had a more general sense than that of the strict relationship and in Egypt the Ptolemies called their wives 'sisters' even if they were not, as they often were, in that blood-relationship to them. The papyri also provide examples of the terms used to one another by members of religious communities (cf. Matt. 23.8: YOU HAVE ONE TEACHER, AND YOU ARE ALL BRETHREN), and here as elsewhere in the New Testament the word means simply 'a believer', 'a Christian', a member of the same family of God.

brethren of the Lord

from their position here these were evidently of some standing in the Church; 'the casual reference to them,' comments Moffatt (p. 116) 'is another reminder of how much was going on in the primitive period of which we have little or no information in the New Testament writings. . . . The only one familiar to us is James and even the record of his conversion is obscure.' For an extended note see Goudge (p. 74).

14. St Paul would have in mind such injunctions as Matt. 10.10 and Luke 10.7 f. The strength of his feeling on the matter is shown in that he is unshaken in his decision although the practice had dominical sanction. It is important to note, in connection with his reference to this, that the traditions of the Church, as early as this, included one of the Lord's own provision for and expectation of the carrying on of his apostolic work of preaching the gospel.

19-23. Accustomed as he was to misunderstanding, St Paul proceeds to enunciate a principle that he must have known to be open to attack as 'compromise' or 'the line of least resistance'. But what he says is vital to the propagation of the gospel. The Christian preacher must go to the utmost lengths, short of surrendering vital principles, to accommodate himself to the traditions and practices of those amongst whom he has to do his work. Thus at risk of being called a coward he had Timothy circumcised and at risk of being called an apostate he had set on one side Jewish food laws. And he does this not in any spirit of easy optimism about the triumphs that are to follow; he does not expect a complete victory. I HAVE BEEN EVERYTHING BY TURNS TO EVERY-BODY (Knox) TO BRING SALVATION TO SOME (v. 22). Knox, following the Vulgate, translates 'to bring everybody salvation', but the MSS support for this is not strong, though early.

20. not under the law

What he means by this is worked out in Galatians and Romans; faith in a Person had for him replaced obedience to a code.

21. to them that are . . . under law to Christ

His experiences at Corinth had taught him the danger of pagan misunderstandings of his teaching about obedience to Christ giving freedom from the law; the Greek word he used, *anomos*, could mean not only 'without law' but 'law-less' and he adds the necessary correction.

24-27. He ends with metaphors from the Isthmian Games familiar to all his readers, and by implication contrasts, as many Christian preachers have done since, the exacting discipline which men were prepared to undergo in these earthly contests with Christian failure to grasp the demands made on those who sought the highest of all prizes, These verses, says Moffatt, 'are a call to rise, at all costs, above what Aristotle once described as the barbarian ideal of living as one likes' (p. 125). Christians are by no means always ready to spend themselves utterly in the pursuit of their heavenly goal; they often seem distressingly vague as to what their objective is; they are inclined to rest upon their oars (to use a metaphor which St Paul did not use) and take their victory for granted. 'Run to win,' says the Apostle; 'keep your eye on your objective; don't be like a boxer beating the air; never relax, for the test is exacting and we, of all men, must ring true.'

27. I myself should be rejected (RV); a castaway (AV); disqualified (Moffatt).

The Greek word, *adokimos*, is a word properly used of coins and metals that do not stand up to the test and are

not approved (cf. Isa. 1.22 and Prov. 25.4 [LXX]); translate
'lest I myself should not ring true'.

THE HISTORY OF ISRAEL AFFORDS A WARNING
AGAINST SPIRITUAL PRIDE

10.1-13

We pass from an illustration from Greek life to one from
the history of the Hebrew people; the latter is of wider
significance for St Paul. He sees in the history of his people
the history of the People of God at an earlier stage. The
true beginning of the Church of God is in the call of Abra-
ham, and the people of the Old Testament are in truth our
fathers in the faith. Their experiences, good or bad, can be
our experiences too; the things that happened to them can
provide us with salutary warnings and examples. They had
their sacraments, as we have. As we pass through the waters
of baptism, so they were baptized in the waters of the over-
shadowing cloud and of the Red Sea; as we feed on the
eucharistic bread, so they fed on the manna. But despite this
sacramental life our fathers fell into sin; they abandoned
self-discipline and self-control; they were discontented,
demanding more privileges from God than they had been
allowed; they turned aside to false gods and, as was to be
expected, idolatry and immorality went hand in hand;
above all they felt completely sure of themselves and certain
of their own righteousness. Terrible punishments befell them
in consequence. The Corinthians must take warning in time.
There must be an end to their overweening self-confidence.
They will have no immunity from temptation, any more
than anyone else has. Their only hope is complete trust and
confidence in God. He has allowed in his world the existence
of evil, and therefore of temptation, but HE KNOWETH
WHEREOF WE ARE MADE (Ps. 103.14) and does not expect

of us what is beyond our powers. 'Temptation is probation, and God orders the temptation in such a way that "ye may be able to endure it". The *power* to endure is given . . .; the endurance is not given; that depends on ourselves' (ICC, p. 209).

4. that spiritual food . . . drink . . . rock

The Greek word for 'spiritual' is *pneumatikos*, a word which the New Testament charged with meanings of its own, enriching and enlarging its original connotation of having to do with the wind or breath. Thus it is especially the adjective denoting the rational part of man, that which is akin to God. It is further developed to mean 'belonging to a spirit or to a being higher than man', and then more particularly to things emanating from, or to persons wholly under the influence of the Holy Spirit. From this comes the further sense applied to things or events wholly due to divine action by God himself, and hence it can mean 'supernatural'. This is the translation of it given here by RSV and Moffatt, as against 'spiritual' in AV and RV, and there is no doubt that it is much the better translation. Knox, however, translates it as 'prophetic', claiming in a footnote that though the 'sense may be merely that of "supernatural", it seems more likely that St Paul is regarding the manna, the water and the rock as types of things to come.' He quotes in support Rev. 11.8: THE GREAT CITY WHICH *pneumatikōs*, i.e., PROPHETICALLY, IS CALLED SODOM. In view of the place amongst SPIRITUAL GIFTS ascribed by St Paul to prophecy (see 14.1 ff.), Knox's translation seems attractive.

rock that followed them

There is, no doubt, in St Paul's mind a rabbinical fable about a rock following the Israelites and supplying them with water, but the words following show that he did not accept such a story literally.

and the rock was Christ

We have already noticed (8.6) St Paul's acceptance, as part of the Christian tradition, of the belief in Christ's part in creation; here his pre-existence is referred to in passing as a belief in no way calling for justification; it was part of what Christians held in common. Philo had already said that the rock was the Wisdom of God;[1] perhaps St Paul had met this view. He has already identified Christ with Wisdom (see note on 2.6); and here he says that THE ROCK in the wilderness *WAS* CHRIST. The source of the water that gave the Israelites life was none other than Christ himself, who, in the new dispensation, was himself to be the WATER OF LIFE (Rev. 21.6), and was to feed with the BREAD OF LIFE (John 6.35) the children of those fathers who, in the wilderness, after being BAPTIZED IN THE CLOUD AND IN THE SEA, had fed upon that BREAD WHICH THE LORD had GIVEN them TO EAT (Ex. 16.15). A number of Old Testament references follow, mentioning incidents in the journeyings of the Israelites recorded in Exodus and Numbers. Note once again the persistence of the link between idolatry and fornication (vv. 7 f.). Cf. Wisd. 14.12: THE DEVISING OF IDOLS WAS THE BEGINNING OF FORNICATION.

11. upon whom the ends of the ages are come (RV)

'In whom history has reached its fulfilment' (Knox). Possibly this may mean that the Christian age is the final age of the world; all other ages were preparatory to it (Goudge). Or it may mean either that each age in its turn is completed and summed up, and the sum total has come down to us for whom it was intended; or that the ends of the ages have reached us, and therefore we are already in a new age which is the final one, and the time will be short (ICC). In the general context of I Corinthians, this last seems the most convincing; the sense of urgency which we noted in connection with St Paul's advice on marriage is

[1] *Allegories of the Laws*, II, 86.

still with us, and the Corinthians are being exhorted to take to heart quickly the warnings and examples of the Scriptures.

THERE IS A REAL POSSIBILITY OF COMMUNION WITH THE EVIL ENTITIES WHICH THE IDOLS REPRESENT

10.14-22

The thought of the manna in the wilderness leads on to the thought of the true Bread from heaven, the Eucharist, and the Apostle sees in that, and in the intimate communion which is there brought about between Christians and their Lord and with each other, the final impossibility of sharing in sacrificial acts with the heathen. This last act just cannot be 'a mere nothing, an empty ceremony', for behind the empty idol is the evil power which it represents. In his efforts at reconciliation, St Paul is really conceding the truth in both points of view. Those who treat the whole thing as meaningless are right up to a point, but they have not allowed sufficiently for the existence of evil spiritual powers, THE RULERS OF THE DARKNESS OF THIS WORLD (Eph. 6.12). So, too, those are right who see the eating of idol-meats as something to be totally avoided; but their error is to attribute to the idols themselves a reality which they do not possess. What makes it imperative to avoid heathen sacrificial occasions is the belief, firmly held even by devout Jewish monotheists like St Paul himself, that evil demonic powers really existed, and that communion with them through the sacrificial meal was really possible. If this were so, no Christian must ever partake of them, for he has his own sacrifice through which he has communion in Christ with the one true God. (Note that it is actual sacrificial meals with which the Apostle is dealing here; in vv. 23 ff.

he is dealing with something different, and is not being self-contradictory as is sometimes suggested; he is merely returning there to an aspect of the problem which he had already touched on, in 8.7 ff., from a somewhat different angle.)

16. There is no special significance in placing THE CUP first (cf. 11.23 f.); the Apostle is thinking more of the general similarities between Christian and heathen sacrificial meals than of ritual details. The two main points which he wishes to make are first, as we have seen, the reality of communion, through sacrifice, with the Being or beings to whom the sacrifice is offered, and secondly, the essential unity between the worshippers which partaking in the sacrifice creates; with the implication, once more emphasized, that the Corinthians, since they are Christians, must not act as if they are separate individuals. The Eucharist is the food of those who are at baptism incorporated into Christ, and by partaking of it, they become MEMBERS ONE OF ANOTHER, for

17. the one bread makes us one body, though we are many in number; the same bread is shared by all

In the next chapter St Paul returns again to the Eucharist, but we may note here not only that it is for him the sacrament of unity, but that he can take for granted its central place in the worshipping life of the Christian community; and also that it is interpreted in terms of sacrifice involving a real and not merely symbolical sharing in the sacrifice of the Body and Blood of Christ, through the bread and wine of the Eucharist.

The tradition of the Institution of the Eucharist which had been handed down to St Paul (see 11.23) included the words THIS IS MY BODY; and these words must have been a formative element in his thinking about the Church as the Body of Christ. THE BREAD WHICH WE BREAK, IS IT NOT A PARTICIPATION IN THE BODY OF CHRIST? These words carry with them the meaning of a sharing not only in all that

happens to the Church, but also in what happened to the
human body of Jesus, in his suffering, death and resurrection. (Cf. Phil. 3.10 f.; HIM I WOULD LEARN TO KNOW, AND
THE VIRTUE OF HIS RESURRECTION, AND WHAT IT MEANS TO
SHARE HIS SUFFERINGS, MOULDED INTO THE PATTERN OF HIS
DEATH, IN THE HOPE OF ACHIEVING RESURRECTION FROM THE
DEAD: Knox.) But for St Paul, it is not only a question of
'the individual Jesus Christ, but of a corporate personality
whose visible material manifestation is the Church which
is his body'. Hence 'union with Christ finds its expression
in this societary way in membership of the body of Christ'.[1]

At the Eucharist each individual Christian has his own
'encounter' with the Christ, his own personal moment of
communion with God through Christ, which is his alone,
incommunicable; but he has this in the setting of something
which is shared by all. He must needs share, not only in
the fellowship of those who worship with him, but in the
life of Christ, crucified, risen, glorious, as that life is given
through the Holy Spirit to the Church. It is indeed our partaking in the life of the one Body which makes us, many as
we are, one body ourselves, and it is our continuing to
share in the life of that one Body through the Eucharist
that, in the midst of all our multiplicity, secures our unity.
THE ONE BREAD MAKES US ONE BODY, THOUGH WE ARE MANY
IN NUMBER; THE SAME BREAD IS SHARED BY ALL.[2] Cullmann
in his discussion of the washing of the disciples' feet (John
13.1-20), stresses the connection of this incident with the
Eucharist, pointing out the emphasis in v.8. on the Eucharist
as the basis of the fellowship with Christ which is realized
in the Church, and in subsequent verses on the fellowship
of Christians with one another.[3] He holds that the Fourth
Evangelist links the two fellowships closely together, as in

[1] Higgins, p. 69.
[2] For a full treatment of this whole subject, see Thornton, *passim*, and
esp. ch. 11.
[3] *ECW*, p. 107.

this passage (I Cor. 10.16 f.) St Paul links the resurrection body of the exalted Christ with the Christian community.

18. The reality of communion in the Eucharist is borne out not only by the pagan sacrificial ideas with which he is immediately concerned, but also by the sacrifices of the Old Covenant; the sacrifices of the Jews to Yahweh meant that they were Yahweh's people.

22. Furthermore, their history had shown that there could be no divided allegiance; the one God by his very nature demands and must demand whole-hearted and uncompromising service.

GUIDING PRINCIPLES ON THIS ISSUE

10.23–11.1

St Paul now returns to the kind of question about idol-meats with which he was engaged in ch. 8. He has meanwhile absolutely forbidden Corinthian participation in heathen sacrificial meals, a difficult enough ruling for Christians involved in social or public life. But in less directly compromising cases he is prepared to be lenient. Food may be bought in the shops without question as to its source of origin. Food may also be eaten in private houses without question, unless the idolatrous source from which it has been obtained is directly named by some scrupulous Christian. In such a case the principle enunciated in 8.9 f., illustrated in ch. 9 and repeated in 10.23 f., must come into play; Christian liberty is no individualistic thing; it must be enjoyed in a fellowship and is limited by considerations of the well-being of others. All Christians know they are free; all Christians know that everything there is is created by God. Despite all this, tender consciences must be respected. It is for God's glory we must do everything, and in aiming at this there must often be self-sacrifice and surrender even of what one may legitimately claim, that others may be saved. Such self-sacrifice has been the Apostle's guiding principle, and he has learnt it from Christ.

28. if someone says to you

This SOMEONE may be either the host or some scrupulous fellow-Christian guest. Probably the latter, for a pagan host (and the context requires that he should be pagan) is hardly likely to 'have a conscience' about food that had been offered to idols.

29. Possibly with his own circumcision of Timothy in mind, a thing to which he had consented for charity's sake, only to have it interpreted as a sign of weakness, St Paul insists that concessions made in this way are in no way a surrender of one's freedom.

30. The grace one says over meat of any kind recognizes it as God's creation and one is free to eat it, but it will not be of much benefit to assert one's liberty in this way and put oneself in a false position in the eyes of one's fellow-Christians.

11.1. This verse is best understood as by St Chrysostom (quoted by Moffatt, p. 145): 'Nothing is so effective in making one imitate Christ as caring for one's neighbour.'

VII

PROBLEMS CONNECTED WITH PUBLIC WORSHIP

11.2-34

It would appear (12.1) that the Corinthians had asked for guidance in connection with the exercise of SPIRITUAL GIFTS at the worship of the Church. But before dealing with the specific problems raised in the Corinthians' question, St Paul proceeds first to raise with them two other matters about which he is displeased, in connection with their conduct of public worship. In 11.2-16 he discusses the veiling of women in public worship, and in 11.17-34 disorders and abuses in connection with the Eucharist.

THE VEILING OF WOMEN

11.2-16

It is the Apostle's misfortune that many who know nothing else about him have a vague idea that he was anti-feminist, liked women to have their hair long, and insisted on their having their heads covered in church. It is a minor irony that many who would be baffled by a simple question on the Incarnation, and have probably never heard of justi-fication or of the atonement, were still, until quite recent days, long after their religion had become vestigial, reluc-tant to enter a church building without putting a handker-chief or similar object on the heads of their women-folk.

No doubt in this section of I Corinthians the Apostle reveals himself as a child of his times. Rabbinical exegesis of the Scriptures, and particularly the second and more primitive of the creation stories in Genesis, odd floating legends about angels, and childhood memories, all played a part in influencing what he writes here. But amongst it all it is possible to find certain principles of permanent value for the Church and we must always remember that in estimating his contribution to the discussion or elucidation of any subject we should look at no passage in isolation but in the context of his whole teaching.

His attitude on the position of women in church was not a fixed one. He had enunciated early the great principle of sex-equality: IN CHRIST THERE IS NEITHER JEW NOR GREEK, MALE NOR FEMALE, BOND NOR FREE (Gal. 3.28). But his background was sometimes too much for him. His rabbinical training, his early life in Tarsus (where all decent women veiled), his experiences in Corinth itself, where exotic types of religion much favoured by women flourished with much grave scandal, and where what we might call 'the emancipated woman' was a common sight, all seem to have kept recurring to his mind. The ministry of such women as Lydia and Chloe and Phoebe and Priscilla, and the praise he gives them, is sufficient evidence that he was no anti-feminist, but he was particularly anxious that Christianity should not be classed in the public mind with those popular types of religion in which women took a prominent and far from modest part. While he honoured women of good and noble life, and approved of their prominence in the Church, he was conservative on the question of feminine liberty of action, and insisted on the need for observing proper modesty. His fundamental position is clear: he would not have sanctioned any refusal of full opportunities of service to women in their own sphere. But it is also clear that he would not have agreed that there is *no* difference between men and women. There is no doubt in his mind that there is an *equality of status* before Christ; but he sees that there is a *difference of function*. It is this kind of principle that governs his attitude to marriage and divorce and enables him to write so wisely about the family (Col. 3 and Eph. 6).

2. In this reference to TRADITIONS we have one more bit of evidence for the existence even at this early stage of codes of Christian conduct and credal and liturgical formularies (cf. 15.3-7; I Tim. 3.16).

3. The principle is asserted of a kind of hierarchy in creation itself, which feminine behaviour in Corinth is setting on one side.

4. dishonoureth his head
i.e., if the man were to veil his head he would seem to be acknowledging some superior authority, whereas it is Christ alone whom he should acknowledge as Master and Lord. In view of 14.34-37 we shall probably be right in thinking that St Paul is here thinking of more or less private activities of this kind. The occasion would be something more than 'family prayers' for it is hardly likely, for example, that the four daughters of Philip the Evangelist, who are described in Acts 21.9 as PROPHESYING, confined this activity to the family circle. But the trouble at Corinth was with people who wished to discard the veiling of women in public and who may well have wished the gift of prophesying, when they possessed it, to be exercised in the public worship of the Church, which would hardly have been possible without unveiling.

5-7. dishonoureth her head
i.e., she flouts the order of nature itself and might as well go the whole way and be shaved (the punishment of an adulteress).

8-10. The Apostle emphasizes the significance of the order in which creation itself proceeded.

because of the angels

If we follow Tertullian we have here a reference to evil angels and the story of Gen. 6.1-4; women must remember that not only men but even angels can be tempted by them. If we do not follow him, the reference is to the participation of angels in the worship of the Church, and the woman is urged to remember that careless behaviour on our part will shock not only her fellow human beings but angels as well.

power over her head

A strange phrase, which *may* mean the security and dignity given a woman by her veil; without it she becomes one whom any man may feel free to insult and despise.

11. A re-assertion of the complete dependence of man and woman upon one another which St Paul had already proclaimed in connection with marriage; his strong sense of their 'equality in Christ' is really too much for his rabbinical upbringing.

13-16. After an appeal to their sense of natural propriety he ends (v. 16) by telling the Corinthians that whether they agree with what he has said or not, they should remember that they are not the whole Church of God; they must not ignore apostolic authority and the universal practice of their fellow-Christians. Once again we see what a hard lesson for the Corinthians to learn was their membership of the catholic Church and all that it implied.

H

THE EUCHARIST

11.17-34

The Apostle is still unable to answer the direct question he was asked, for he has heard of further scandals in Corinthian worship; this time in connection with the Eucharist itself. As we have seen, there is some New Testament evidence for a common meal which preceded or may have been a kind of preliminary part of the Eucharist proper. Such meals were a commonplace in the guild life of the times and were one of the means of promoting fellowship between guild members. For Christians this meal corresponded to the meal in the Upper Room, and it was to re-enact this meal, with its culmination in the Eucharist, that they met. 'The whole purpose of the gathering was to take part in the Lord's Supper as enacted by our Lord with his disciples.'[1] Unfortunately some of the Christians at Corinth were behaving in a way which entirely destroyed the significance of the whole event. There was class-feeling (cf. James 2.1-4); there were private cliques; the better-off, who provided the food and drink, started at once without waiting for the rest (probably slaves and artisans who were delayed by their work), and that to such a purpose that gluttony and drunkenness were not unknown, while late-comers went hungry. All this kind of thing, the Apostle tells them, makes the ostensible object for which they came together unreal; a supper is eaten indeed, but it is not the *Lord's* Supper and might just as well, or even better, have been eaten at home. It is a denial of the whole meaning of the Church and involves grave dangers for them all. The nature of these he proceeds to explain, introducing what he has to say by a recapitulation of the institution of the

[1] Thornton, p. 334.

Eucharist which he had already given them as part of the apostolic tradition.

18. *Schismata* and (19) *haireseis*; neither of these words has as yet developed its formal meaning: we must not think of ' schism ' or of ' heresy '. At Corinth there are only dissensions and cliques within the church. Translate, with Phillips, I HEAR THAT YOU SPLIT UP INTO SMALL GROUPS. . . . FOR THERE MUST BE CLIQUES AMONG YOU.

19. I suppose there must needs be

A facing of the inevitable in a fallen world. Compare our Lord's similar words, IT MUST NEEDS BE THAT OFFENCES COME (Matt. 18.7). ' Genuine ' (*dokimoi*) Christians are soon detected in such circumstances, for they remain apart from the parties and the quarrels.

22. Or are you prepared to bring the Church of God into contempt by the embarrassment you inflict on its poor?

The implication is plainly that the Corinthians, in despising the poor Christians, THE LITTLE ONES of this world who believe in Christ, are actually bringing Christ himself into contempt in THE CHURCH, WHICH IS HIS BODY. Here lies the real sin of the Corinthians, they have failed to realize the meaning of their baptism, by which they are incorporated into Christ and become members of his Body.

23-26. In these verses we have our earliest account of the origin of the Eucharist, and as Jeremias[1] and Cullmann[2] have shown, what St Paul gives us has reached him as an already existing liturgical form. THE LORD, says Cullmann, in passages like this (cf. I Cor. 7.10, 25; I Thess. 4.15) is a phrase which is equivalent to ' the tradition of the apostolic

[1] *The Eucharistic Words of Jesus*, p. 107.
[2] ' Kyrios ', *Scottish Journal of Theology*, June 1950.

Church', seen as the voice of the living Christ; the solemn
formula THE LORD JESUS is a liturgical confession of faith
(cf. I Cor. 12.3 and Rom. 10.9); the words IN THE NIGHT IN
WHICH HE WAS BETRAYED are not merely a chronological
statement; they refer to an action of God and perhaps of
our Lord himself, and not just to the betrayal by Judas.
Comparing this account with those in the Evangelists we
find common to them all the Taking of the Bread and the
Cup, the Giving of Thanks, the Breaking of the Bread, the
words TAKE; THIS IS MY BODY and THIS IS MY BLOOD OF THE
COVENANT WHICH IS POURED OUT FOR MANY. There are also
common to the four accounts the sacrificial atmosphere in
which the rite is celebrated and the eschatological note,
struck here with the words YOU PROCLAIM THE LORD'S
DEATH, TILL HE COMES (cf. Mark 14.25; Matt. 26.29; Luke 22.
15-18). Peculiar to St Paul (and to St Luke if we accept the
longer version) are the words PERFORM THIS ACTION AS MY
MEMORIAL (but cf. Moffatt, p. 166: 'The probability is that
the eucharist in the love-feast was so regular a feature of
Church life, when the Gospels were written, that its repeti-
tion could be taken for granted. In which case, Paul would
be no more than making explicit what was implicit in the
other traditions'). What the Apostle may well have been
first to do, by his direction that hungry Christians had better
eat at home, was to take the first step which was later to
result, first in the complete separation of the *agape* or
community-Meal from the Eucharist, and finally in its disappearance, except for vestigial remains such as the *eulogia*
in the East and the *pain bénit* in the West.

23. in which he was betrayed

Better, translate with ICC 'in which he was being delivered up', or with Jeremias[1] 'in the night in which God
delivered him up', which brings out the significance of the
betrayal as part of the divine plan (cf. Acts 2.23: BY GOD'S

[1] *Eucharistic Words*, p. 107.

FIXED DESIGN AND FOREKNOWLEDGE, HE WAS BETRAYED TO
YOU: Knox).

25. in remembrance of me

These words are of far wider application than to the
death of Christ only; they include the whole scheme of
redemption culminating in the resurrection, the immense
importance of which is reflected in the selection of the first
day of the week for the continuance of the memorial. Christ
spiritually present at the Eucharist is the risen Christ. It is
a commemoration not only of the atoning death but of the
meals eaten with the risen Lord in the Easter passover
(cf. Acts 10.41: WE DID EAT AND DRINK WITH HIM AFTER HE
ROSE FROM THE DEAD).

26. Proclaim the Lord's death till he come

The Greek verb translated 'proclaim' has a note of
triumph about it, for it is the Lord's death that is the beginning of the new order of salvation. The Eucharist is full
of the sense of the coming of Christ, a coming which is at
once past, present and future; it is a coming in the spiritual
order, where the past is brought into the present and the
future is anticipated. *Maranatha*, the Aramaic word quoted
at the end of this epistle, is a eucharistic word; no Eucharist
was celebrated without eager looking forward to the coming
of the Son of Man: EVEN SO COME, LORD JESUS was the
earnest prayer of every devout communicant.

24-32. We now turn from the origin of the Eucharist to its
significance. If we compare vv. 17-34 and 10.16-22, we
cannot escape the conclusion that for St Paul, and therefore also for the 'tradition' which he had received, there is
a real giving of the life of the Lord in the Eucharist and a
real presence in it of the Lord's body. 'Jesus is making over
to his followers, "till he come", his actual self, his life and
personality' (Robinson, p. 57). These two truths are not

created by human faith; they are the work of the Holy Spirit in the Church, for all Christian worship since the resurrection is worship in the Spirit. The 'means of grace' replace the Temple, the sacrificial system, even the sabbath itself. Neither in Mount Gerizim nor in Jerusalem is Christian worship any longer confined, and TRUE WORSHIPPERS NOW WORSHIP THE FATHER IN SPIRIT AND TRUTH. The life of the Lord, and the real presence thus brought to them by the Spirit, have both to be grasped by faith, and it is the tragedy of the Corinthian Christians that despite their many spiritual gifts they are wanting in the faith that is vital to their spiritual well-being, and have brought themselves under the judgment of God. The rich complexity of the phrase THE LORD'S BODY embraces the thoughts of the body sacrificed on Calvary, of the glorified resurrection body and of the Mystical Body, the Church, in which Christ lives on in those who have been baptized into his Body. The Corinthians' conduct shows that they have failed in their grasp of the significance of all these. The principle of sacrifice has eluded them; the vital union between them and the risen body has not been understood (see 10.16 f.); they have not grasped that Christ and his Church are one, and that in despising their fellow-Christians they are despising Christ. A. E. J. Rawlinson[1] thinks that the description of the Church as THE BODY OF CHRIST ('this very remarkable phrase') owes its origin to the use of the same phrase in connection with the Eucharist, as for example in 10.17 of this epistle.

It is, of course, to St Paul that we owe the development of the conception of the Church as the Body of Christ, as 'the extension of the life and person of the incarnate Christ beyond his resurrection and ascension' (Robinson, p. 57). He arrived at it no doubt by more than one way, of which the most obvious are the words of institution themselves, and his vision of the risen Lord with the words I AM JESUS

[1] *The New Testament Doctrine of the Christ*, 1926, p. 157 n.

WHOM THOU PERSECUTEST (Acts 26.15). He did not invent
the conception, for he seems, for example in 6.15, to be able
to take for granted Corinthian understanding of what he was
talking about. Moreover we may recall the Allegory of the
Sheep and the Goats in Matt. 25.31-46, with the words
INASMUCH AS YE DID IT TO THE LEAST OF THESE MY BRETHREN
YE DID IT UNTO ME. In the Johannine tradition the Allegory
of the Vine and the Branches teaches the same truths.

25. We have already seen in 5.7 a glance back at the ancient
passover feast of the Jews, now replaced by the true Paschal
Lamb; here we look for a moment at the day of atonement,
whose hopes and strivings are now fulfilled in him who
ratifies a new covenant between God and man and estab-
lishes final and full communion between them. The best
commentary is in Heb. 9.11 f.: BUT WHEN CHRIST APPEARED
AS A HIGH PRIEST OF THE GOOD THINGS THAT HAVE COME
. . . HE ENTERED IN ONCE FOR ALL INTO THE HOLY PLACE,
TAKING NOT THE BLOOD OF GOATS AND CALVES BUT HIS OWN
BLOOD, THUS SECURING AN ETERNAL REDEMPTION (RSV).

27. Translate, with RSV, WILL BE GUILTY OF PROFANING
THE BODY AND BLOOD OF OUR LORD.

28. let a man examine himself
The Greek verb is associated with the testing of metals,
or with the passing of examinations; here it means: 'Let
him look carefully into the sincerity of his professions.'

29-34. There follows in the Greek text a play upon a number of words associated with judging, examining, condemning and the like, impossible to reproduce in English. Over
the whole passage is the atmosphere of judgment, of final
decisions, of a relationship between our actions now and
the temporal judgments they incur, and the final judgment
of the Messiah with whose body and blood Christians are

so vitally linked by the Cross, by the Lord's Table, by the Church.

29. not discerning, or distinguishing, or rightly judging the Lord's body

This phrase means that unworthy communicants show by their attitude and conduct that 'they do not recognize the Lord's body for what it is': i.e., either they completely fail to recognize the nature of the Eucharistic presence and the sacrificial nature of the gift and the demands there made: or they do not see in their fellow-communicants the presence of the Christ himself. Their gluttony and their drunkenness are bad enough, but worse is their failure of charity, for this blinds them to the unity of the Church as the Lord's Body; they do not see that THE ONE BREAD MAKES US ONE BODY. Consequently they eat so as to incur God's 'punishment' (in v. 29 this is the word rather than 'condemnation' or 'damnation'). The reference is not to the hereafter, but to the temporal punishments which many of them have already experienced, as illustrated in v. 30. Such punishments are God's judgments; they are not his final condemnation, but warnings to lead them to repentance in time, to save them from the doom that awaits THE WORLD—i.e., 'humanity in its present state, alienated from its maker'.[1]

33.

The Apostle sums up what he has been saying in a few practical words; love and fellowship must be regained and exemplified in kindly and courteous conduct to one another; without these, sacraments will not save them.

34. the rest will I set in order when I come

'One may guess for ever, and without result, as to what things the Apostle was going to set in order' (ICC).

[1] B. F. Westcott, *The Gospel according to St John* (1908), additional note on 1.10, Vol. 1, p. 65.

WHAT OF SPIRITUAL GIFTS? AND HOW ARE
THEY TO BE EXERCISED IN PUBLIC WORSHIP

12.

In the background of these chapters is St Paul's view of
the nature of the universe. He accepts, as our Lord did,
what we would call a dualistic view. He sees the world as
the scene of a struggle between great invisible forces of good
and evil. The troubles of the world, its sin, its suffering, are
the work of evil spirits. They have got hold of man in what
St Paul calls his ' flesh ', a word by which he means our
whole lower nature, which is consequently caught up in sin,
that profound disorder of a spiritual kind involving not only
man but the whole universe. Unlike Oriental myths which
set this great struggle in the past, or Jewish speculations
which put it in the future, St Paul sets it in the present, and
sees man as an inevitably a combatant in the struggle. But
it is, of course, a limited dualism that St Paul accepts; there
is no question of where victory lies; for St Paul, as for all
Christians, the resurrection of Christ has set the issue beyond
all doubt; the last word is with LIFE AND GOOD and not with
DEATH AND EVIL (cf. Deut. 30.15). Nevertheless, the struggle
while it lasts is real and terrible, and the good will have
many setbacks. But St Paul believed, as has been well said,
not in the inevitability of progress, but in the invincibility
of divine love. As Dr Dodd has pointed out, he did *not* say,
ALL THINGS WORK TOGETHER FOR GOOD TO THEM THAT LOVE
GOD, but GOD CO-OPERATES WITH THEM THAT LOVE HIM IN
ALL RESPECTS FOR GOOD. It is this view of the universe that
we must have in our minds, when we try to understand both
Corinthian questions such as are implied in 12.3, and also
St Paul's own assumptions about the evil spiritual influences
behind idol-worship and sacrifices, which are made explicit
in 10.19-22, and which seem to underlie 12.2 as well. A man

exercised good or evil gifts because he was under spiritual
influences corresponding to them, and in extreme cases he
could be ' possessed ' by such influences or beings. It all
seems strange to us (this particular chapter seemed strange
to Christians even as early as St Chrysostom), partly because it is involved with ways of thinking foreign to us,
partly because the phenomena St Paul is dealing with ceased
at an early date to be part of the normal experience of the
Church. But Christian missionaries, and others, who have
resided long in unconverted Africa, for example, often
speak of experiences which very much recall the old pagan
world in which the first Christians moved.[1]

1-3. The Greek word *pneumatikon* (see note on 10.4)
may be here either masculine or neuter, ' persons ' or ' gifts '.
In 14.1 it is obviously neuter, but v. 3 here suggests the masculine. The query will then be, ' What criterion have we for
distinguishing between inspired persons? ' It was a problem
familiar to St Paul who would remember its being posed in
the Old Testament (see, e.g., Jer. 28). The problem re-
appears in the New Testament in I John 4.1 f., where the
test is recognition of Jesus as the Messiah come IN THE
FLESH. St Paul's answer here is twofold; negative and
positive.

2. those dumb idols

The idols were non-entities; here St Paul would agree
with the more enlightened Corinthians; but just as sharing
in sacrifices offered to them was to run the risk of corruption by the evil powers they represented, so here the
Corinthians must be thought of as in their heathen days
having been LED AWAY by the powers behind the idols they
worshipped. The Greek verb has, in the papyri both BC
and AD, the sense of being ' seized ' or ' captured '.

[1] See, for example, *Africa Dances* by Geoffrey Gorer, published as a
Penguin Book in 1945.

3. Jesus is anathema

This is the negative test. If in a trance or ecstatic state a possessed person cries out, JESUS IS ACCURSED, we know at once that his inspiration does not come from God. Such a test seems to us somewhat odd, but we have to allow for a confusion of ecstatic utterances containing all kinds of words and phrases. Evans (p. 129) suggests that it is the possibility in such cases of contradictions and incoherencies that in St Paul's view rules out the possibility of genuine inspiration. It is to be contrasted ' with the orderliness and consistency of the true religion; the Holy Spirit never contradicts himself.'

no man can say . . . but in the Holy Spirit

St Paul here, in giving his positive test, enunciates two truths of the greatest importance, first that a confession of faith of this kind is a gift of God; it is not a discovery of our own but it comes to us from God through the inspiration and guidance of the Holy Spirit (cf. 2.10). Having received this revelation (as St Paul himself had in a specially dramatic way) we proceed, as he did, to baptism and learn what it is to be members of the Body of Christ, his Church in which the Spirit dwells as its life-giving principle. The second truth here implied is that this recognition of Jesus as Lord is not restricted; it is not confined to those possessed of ' special ' gifts of the Spirit; it is God's gift to *all* Christians.

4-11. In this section St Paul faces once again two Corinthian weaknesses—pride and self-satisfaction, and a tendency to rivalries and jealousy. Consequently he emphasizes the truth that all the spiritual gifts they boast of come from the one divine source, the Holy Spirit, and that these gifts are distributed within the Body of Christ, to be used for building it up. His whole argument rests upon belief in the unity of God, the Blessed Trinity. Such theological terms are of course not to be found here, but we have here, and even more clearly in Eph. 4.4-6, one body utterly dependent for its being on the one God and Father of all, dependent on one Lord, with the one Spirit from whom derives its life.[1]

4-6. Different kinds of spiritual endowments (4); capacities for service (5); special powers (6).

7. each one receives his gift from the Spirit for the good of all

8. one learns to speak with wisdom . . . another with knowledge (Knox).

Here St Paul is thinking of the true *sophia*, ' wisdom ', as against the shallow sophistry he had denounced earlier (1.17). WISDOM is the wider term; KNOWLEDGE the power to grasp the principles which wisdom embodies.

9. faith

What is meant here is the kind of FAITH WHICH CAN REMOVE MOUNTAINS and enable a Christian to exercise the ' special powers ' of v. 6, in miracles of healing, for example, or the other gifts referred to in v. 10.

10. prophecy

In our sense of a ' prophetic ministry ' rather than in the sense of foreseeing of the future: DISTINGUISHING BE-TWEEN SPIRITS probably here means more than was in-volved in v. 3, and means a special spiritual capacity for judging the value of utterances or actions claimed as inspired.

11. the gift of tongues

The phenomena of ecstatic speech, specially valued at Corinth, is put by St Paul, no doubt deliberately, at the end

[1] See ICC, p. 262.

of his list; and the reference to the need for interpreting such phenomena prepares the way for his criticism of it as something individualistic and not likely 'to serve the common good' (12.29 and 14.4-23). It is this phrase which gives the clue to the whole situation which St Paul is thinking of here. All the gifts which he enumerates are exercised in the setting of the worship of the Christian Church, culminating in the Eucharist. Because Christian worship is worship 'in the Spirit' the gifts which men bring to it are the 'gifts of the Spirit'. As such they are exercised within the Church and for its good. This is clearly brought out in 14.5, 12, 26, where the AV word EDIFYING has long hidden the truth that everything has to be done for THE BUILDING UP OF THE BODY OF CHRIST, and that this must be the aim to which all worship is directed, that God may be glorified in the Church. This great variety of SPIRITUAL GIFTS was soon to disappear, but as Cullmann has pointed out[1] it was 'the strength of the earlier service of worship that here free working of the Spirit and liturgical restrictiveness still go hand in hand and together serve the one end, the "building up" of the community. . . . Paul was able to bring freedom of the Spirit and the restrictions of the liturgy together in the self-same service because he saw everything in the light of one aim: . . . the usual alternative, charismatic *or* liturgical worship, is therefore not correct for primitive Christianity.'

12-31. Having spoken of the great diversity of gifts which all proceed from the one God, the Trinity in Unity and Unity in Trinity of later theology, and of these gifts being given to each that they may be used for the good of all, St Paul proceeds to illustrate and further expound what he means by 'the good of all'. It is to be understood in the context of the Church as the Body of Christ. Many and various as are the gifts of the Spirit, those who are given

[1] *ECW*, p. 32.

them are one organic whole, for they are MEMBERS OF CHRIST. They died with him in baptism and they were raised again with him in the resurrection; their life is his life, the risen life which carries in it the conquest of and victory over death. He illustrates it from the human body, a commonplace simile amongst his pagan contemporaries and particularly amongst the Stoics. But this is an illustration only, and must not lead us into supposing that when St Paul speaks of the Church as the Body of Christ he is only dealing in similes. As A. M. Ramsey[1] and Robinson have pointed out, 'to call the Church "the Body of Christ" was to draw attention to it not primarily as a collection of men but primarily as Christ Himself in His own being and life.' Robinson argues (pp. 59-61) that the simile of the human body enables St Paul to solve the problem of how, if the Church *is* the Body of Christ, it can consist of a number of persons. 'All the members of a human body form one body *despite* their number. So it is with the person of Christ.' The unity comes first; the multiplicity follows from it. 'The diversity derives from the pre-existing nature of the unity as organic; it is not a diversity which has to discover or be made into a unity.' Thus the Ephesians (4.3 f.) are urged to keep, to watch, the unity of the one Body, the one Spirit. No doubt St Paul was assisted in his formulation of this doctrine by the readiness with which Hebrew thought accepted the idea of 'corporate personality' or the personification of the faithful remnant, as in the concept of the Suffering Servant or in the Psalms.

13. into one body

i.e., 'the very purpose for which we were baptized was that we should be made into one body.' Thus baptism has the same end as the Eucharist: we partake of the one bread and are sustained in our membership of the one Body.

[1] *The Gospel and the Catholic Church*, p. 35, quoted by Robinson, p. 50.

made to drink

The Greek verb is one of irrigation, of watering. Thus in 3.6 Paul planted the seed of the gospel in Corinth and Apollos WATERED it.

25b-27. These verses drive home the practical application of the simile. What happens to one happens to all, whether it be good or ill; however different their gifts, however many or however few, each separate Corinthian Christian lives only in virtue of his membership of the Body. It was God who made the human body what it is; it is God who is the origin of the Church. In both the principle is the same; no uniformity, infinite variety, but unity above all, unity in the midst of variety, deriving its meaning from the very variety, and securing the latter's permanence.

31. Despite the unity which underlies all, some gifts *are* greater than others, but they all come from God, who distributes them TO EACH MAN SEVERALLY AS HE WILL. We may rightly seek them, but there is something greater than them all, without which they have no value. Even the greatest of them will pass away with this world, but charity will never fail. Moreover, once this is accepted as one's rule of life, ' within its range there can be no thought of self, not even of self as useful to others, but only of the others and of God '.[1]

CHARITY

13.

The same motives, those connected with the associations of the words in question, which led the New Testament writers to choose *agapē* as their word for ' love ', and to reject all the others, influence us in turn to prefer the AV

[1] Evans, p. 133.

'charity' to 'love', the word used by the RV and most
modern translators. The word 'love' in modern ears has
always about it something of the atmosphere of expectancy,
of looking for some return, which it acquires through its
associations with sexual love. The word 'charity', too, has
its restrictions, but at least it retains the element of giving
rather than getting, and of sacrifice and surrender of *something* of one's own, in however small a degree. In the New
Testament it is very much a word in the vocabulary of the
subjects of the Messiah; it will be a word that will still be
used when the kingdoms of this world have passed away;
cf. v. 8: THE TIME WILL COME WHEN WE SHALL OUTGROW
PROPHECY, WHEN SPEAKING WITH TONGUES WILL COME TO
AN END, WHEN KNOWLEDGE SHALL BE SWEPT AWAY; WE
SHALL NEVER HAVE FINISHED WITH CHARITY (Knox) (cf.
Rom. 13.8-10). It is something which comes to us from
the nature of God himself, and brings with it a breath
from the air of eternity; it is 'the divine love poured into
us and overflowing into the lives of others, an "extension"
of God's love for us'.[1] In the Church, indwelt by the Spirit,
Christians have been given BY THE SAME SPIRIT a new vision
and a new experience of the meaning of God's love, and BY
THE SAME SPIRIT a new vision of their fellow-Christians,
and a new power to translate into practice in their day-to-
day life the love of God that they have seen IN THE FACE
OF JESUS CHRIST. Cf. I Thess. 4.9 f.: AS FOR LOVE OF THE
BRETHREN, THERE IS NO NEED TO SEND YOU ANY MESSAGE;
YOU HAVE LEARNED FOR YOURSELVES GOD'S LESSON ABOUT
THE CHARITY YOU OUGHT TO SHEW TO ONE ANOTHER. . . .
WE WOULD ONLY ASK YOU TO MAKE MORE OF IT THAN EVER
(Knox).

1-3. These verses look back to the kind of SPIRITUAL GIFTS
enumerated in 12.8-10.

[1] C. E. B. Cranfield, *TWBB*, p. 135.

3. though I give my body to be burned

This is a phrase that has caused some difficulty, but the most obvious explanation is also the likeliest; martyrdom by fire was something St Paul was perfectly familiar with from his knowledge of the history of Maccabean times; and we may be certain that he had heard of Shadrach, Meshach and Abednego as long ago as he could remember. Even in such drastic self-giving as this, unworthy motives may lie hidden, unless charity governs all.

5. doth not behave itself unseemly

Translate with Phillips HAS GOOD MANNERS.

is not provoked

Again, with Phillips, IS NOT TOUCHY.

taketh not account of evil

The Greek verb refers to the keeping of accounts, and a modern paraphrase might be 'does not file away injuries done to one for further reference'. The kind of thing St Paul had in mind is well illustrated in Fr. James Brodrick's little sketch of Pope Paul IV:[1] 'He never forgot such incidents, which was one of his fundamental weaknesses. He might bury the hatchet for a time, but he gave the impression of always carefully marking the spot.'

6. rejoiceth not over unrighteousness

i.e., is incapable of sympathizing, despite all its tolerance, with the glee of the successful transgressor (ICC).

7.

The general sense is that charity is incurably optimistic and in the most unlikely circumstances keeps on hoping for the best.

8-13.

In his rapturous meditation on charity, St Paul passes,

[1] *Progress of the Jesuits*, 1946, p. 4.

I

in these verses, from its role here on earth in space and
time to its place in the new day that is coming, when
HEAVEN AND EARTH SHALL PASS AWAY, together with everything even of what is best in the temporal order, for it will
be no longer needed.

11. The implication is that 'the gifts of tongues, prophecy
and knowledge themselves belong to the undeveloped stage
of the spiritual life '.[1]

12. Literally translated it runs: ' FOR WE SEE AT PRESENT
BY MEANS OF A MIRROR IN A RIDDLE.' St Paul does not mean
that we are looking into a mirror to see ourselves, but
rather that we can at present only see, as it were reflected
in a mirror, God and the things of God, a simile which gains
added point when we realize that the mirrors he was familiar
with were made only of polished metal, and were much less
efficient than ours. His thought is very similar to that in the
seventh book of the *Republic* of Plato, where our appre-
hension of reality is said to be like that of men sitting in a
cave with their backs to the light of day, only able to guess
at what is going on in the world through reflections and
echoes. Translate, with Phillips, AT PRESENT ALL WE SEE IS
THE BAFFLING REFLECTION OF REALITY IN A MIRROR. But
the simile must not lead us into thinking that knowledge of
God is beyond our power altogether in this world. So far as
is possible for us, we have a *real* knowledge of God, but
it is knowledge ' distorted by falsifying media, by our passions and prejudices and by the passions and prejudices of
other people '.[2]

13. The Apostle has already in this chapter brought charity
into close touch with faith and hope, for CHARITY BELIEVETH
ALL THINGS, HOPETH ALL THINGS (7). They occur together

[1] Goudge, p. 120.
[2] R. L. Nettleship, *Lectures on the Republic of Plato*, 1901, p. 260.

elsewhere throughout the epistles as, for example, I Thess. 5.8, where the Thessalonians are urged to put on THE BREASTPLATE OF FAITH AND CHARITY AND THE HELMET OF HOPE. The point about the word ABIDETH (remaineth) here, is that in the world to come the character built upon these qualities survives; it is carried beyond the Second Advent when the lesser gifts of the Spirit vanish. Perhaps the best comment on this verse, including the words BUT THE GREATEST OF THESE IS CHARITY, is to be found in St Thomas Aquinas:[1] 'Faith . . . is of the intellect; . . . hope is the soul in desire or aspiration; love, the soul in process of achievement. And faith and hope are subsidiary to love, just as intellect and desire should be subordinated to (but not obliterated by) purpose, for love . . . is the bond of perfectness.' Moreover, in the context of this epistle we cannot ignore the position of charity as the supreme essential principle in the life of the Church, securing for the exercise of all other gifts the pursuit of their proper ends, the love of God and the building up of the Church.

THE APOSTLE RETURNS TO THE QUESTION OF SPIRITUAL GIFTS AND THEIR EXERCISE

14.

1-19. He first discusses the comparative value of two gifts in particular, SPEAKING WITH TONGUES and PROPHESYING. Here, as in everything, charity must be the regulative principle and this they must persistently follow. They are, at the same time, to be in no doubt about the value of the spiritual gifts which they have been discussing, but charity will secure that they will seek them only in the context of

[1] Paraphrased by K. E. Kirk, *Some Principles of Moral Theology*, 1920, p. 42.

the well-being of the Church (v. 12). Hence, although St
Paul recognizes SPEAKING WITH TONGUES as a spiritual gift,
and thanks God for his own possession of it to a pre-
eminent degree (v. 18), he also recognizes it as a highly
individualistic thing which may be of little or no service to
the Church. Consequently it is a gift plainly inferior to that
of prophecy. What is this strange religious phenomenon,
' glossolalia ', as it came to be called in the nineteenth century? Acts 2.4 ff. and some of the Fathers take it to mean
a special gift of languages for evangelism, but (a) we have
no record of its being used for such a purpose; and (b) it
would have been unnecessary, for in the context of the
primitive preaching of the Gospel a knowledge of Greek
and Aramaic would have been sufficient; (c) as this verse
itself tells us, no one understood it, and this view of it is
confirmed by Acts 2.13 and v. 23 of this chapter, where it
is ascribed to drunkennes or madness. It is a phenomenon
not unknown in periods of religious revival, though it
quickly dies out, as it did in the early Church. It consists of
ecstatic utterances and cries, sometimes under the control
of the individual, sometimes not, and, if St Luke and St
Paul are concerned with the same phenomenon, evidently
including words or phrases recognizable as in the vocabulary of different languages. (It should be noted, however,
that Moulton and Milligan give evidence to show that *glossa*
need not mean so much a language as a sub-dialect of one.)
It was evidently a showy gift, commanding a good deal of
attention, and, perhaps by many in a place like Corinth,
coveted as a special sign of spirituality. Possibly Old Testa-
men prophecies amongst early Christian proof-texts, such
as Joel 2.28 f., added to its prestige. But from this chapter
we can see that its exercise was by no means approved by
all, and St Paul has to warn such critics against too rigid
an attitude. It is a gift of the Spirit, of that he is sure, but
it is not amongst the greatest, and its careless or persistent
exercise without relation to the well-being of the Church as

a whole can be not only useless but a positive nuisance.
It can be like a musical instrument played without knowledge, a tune with no significance.

2. mysteries

Here used in its ordinary sense; a secret unrevealed.

4. edifieth

Translate BUILDS UP. The kind of prophet here thought of
is not the seer who claims to foretell the future, but he who
knows the things of God and can convey them to men in
words of insight, strength and courage.

12. Here is the centre of all St Paul has to say on this
subject: SINCE, THEN, YOU ARE AMBITIOUS FOR SPIRITUAL
GIFTS, TRY TO EXCEL IN THEM, WITH THE BUILDING UP OF
THE CHURCH AS YOUR AIM.

14. my mind is unfruitful

i.e., it does no good to others; its normal functions, both
of understanding and of explanation, are in suspense while
the ecstasy lasts.

16. he who occupies the place of the unlearned

The Greek word for 'unlearned' is *idiotes,* the private individual as opposed to the official; here it means one without the gift of tongues, and the word can best be translated
as 'the ordinary man'. 'The outsider' (Moffatt) will scarcely
do, especially with its recent new connotation, though it is
just possible that St Paul is talking of someone not a Christian who is present at a Christian service, perhaps from a
wish to learn about this new religion. But in view of vv.
19-25 below, this is hardly likely.

bless with the Spirit

As the context shows, this means thanksgivings offered

in ecstasy. There can hardly be here a specific reference to
the Eucharist.

Amen

This Jewish liturgical word was taken over into Christianity and was said by the congregation assisting, alike at
the more solemn or 'set' parts of the service, and at 'extempore' prayer and spiritual exercises. 'For the most
part such expressions have with us lost their force. They
have become like coins worn smooth by too long usage. But
in the primitive liturgy they have still their pristine fresh-
ness. "Amen!" "So be it!"': uttered by the faithful after
receiving their communion is an act of faith; spoken at
the end of a prayer, it proclaims their solemn acceptance of
the words spoken by the bishop.'[1]

19-25. The superiority of PROPHECY to TONGUES is further
argued. We have already seen that SPEAKING WITH TONGUES
was not of much use or significance to the ordinary Christian. Here we learn that it would be of even less use to the
enquiring or curious pagan who might chance to be present
at Christian worship and to witness such phenomena. Indeed, it might well be that he would depart with a shrug
of the shoulders, with the verdict, 'These people are all
mad.' How different the effect on such a man of a prophet,
a Christian devoutly expounding the word of God and using
it as SOMETHING ALIVE, FULL OF ENERGY . . . QUICK TO
DISTINGUISH EVERY THOUGHT AND DESIGN IN OUR HEARTS
(Heb. 4.12, Knox). Then, pagan though he was, he would
recognize the divine inspiration behind the prophetic
ministry. Despite his recently expressed thanks for his own
gift of tongues St Paul in these verses deals harshly with it.
He suggests it is a gift of the immature and a cause of
childish jealousies, and, by a somewhat perverse exegesis
of Isa. 28.11, declares that in the past the invasion of God's

[1] F. Cabrol, *La Prière des Premiers Chrétiens*, Paris, 1929, pp. 176 f.

people by strangers speaking tongues they could not understand had actually been a punishment inflicted on them for their rejection of prophecy.

26-33. St Paul goes on to give brief directions for worship. Everything must be ordered in accordance with the proper answer to the question, 'What is the purpose of all this?' and the answer is: 'The building up of the Church' (26). This can only be done by a subordination of private gifts to the general good, and by the recognition of the need for order and reverence in the worship of him whom creation reveals as the author of all peace and harmony.

26. This verse provides us with a summary of several elements in Christian worship at this early stage: it included praise (PSALMS, a word more general than our normal use suggests), lessons, prophetic discourses and extempore prayer which might easily pass into ecstasies or trances. But the enthusiasm so obviously present at this early Christion worship must be strictly controlled. TONGUES, that obviously private personal experience, 'a sort of spiritual soliloquy addressed partly to self, partly to Heaven' (ICC, note on 14.2) must not be allowed at all unless there is someone there to make them intelligible. And PROPHETS, too, must learn to consider one another, to avoid being carried away by the urgency of what they have to say, to use their great gift always and only for the service of the Church (v. 31), and to accept the discipline of having the genuineness of their claims to divine guidance tested by their fellows (v. 29).

33. As is the rule in all churches of the saints

This may go either with the preceding or with the following verses. Probably it goes with the preceding, for in v. 34 we have the phrase IN THE CHURCHES again. In either case it is one more warning and reminder to the Corinthians that they exist as a church only because they are members of *the* Church. We have had one such reminder already in 11.16, and another follows almost immediately in v. 36 of this chapter.

34-37. It does not seem necessary to suppose that these verses are out of order or indeed out of place altogether. They do not contradict 11.4 on our interpretation of that passage. The Apostle is here dealing with something different, a proposal that women, or at least married women, should take a full part in those parts of the Christian meetings for worship that were concerned with, for example, the INTERPRETATION OF TONGUES, or discussion of prophetic utterances. Such a proposal would in any case have been hard for one with his background to accept, but in the particular context of Corinth he found it impossible. Once again, too, the Corinthians were forging ahead on their own, forgetting that they were but a part of a larger whole. 16.21 shows us that the letter was dictated, and the reference in 14.33 to ALL THE CHURCHES might well have brought back to his mind the tendency to individualism on the subject of the place of women in the Christian community which was to be found in the Corinthian Church, with this short parenthesis in consequence.

37 f. St Paul asserts his apostolic authority. As the bringer of the gospel to Corinth, he comes to them with THE WORD OF GOD (v. 36) and a COMMANDMENT FROM THE LORD (v. 37). All true prophets, and all possessed of true spiritual gifts, will recognize this and acknowledge his authority for what it is. Those who fail in this recognition will be shown up for what they are, men whose claims to prophecy or inspiration may be disregarded. This interpretation is based on the RV marginal reading, BUT IF ANY MAN KNOWETH NOT, HE IS NOT KNOWN. If we accept the reading in the RV text, then St Paul accepts the condition of ignorance in those who fail to recognize his claims as a fact about which nothing can be done. It may be that on this view we have one more reminder that the time is short and change is no longer possible; men can no longer recede from the position which they have chosen to take up (cf. Rev. 22.11, HE THAT IS WICKED, LET HIM GO ON IN HIS WICKEDNESS). But this is here a somewhat strained interpretation.

40. The chapter closes with the re-assertion of two of its main themes. The gift of prophecy is one to be greatly longed for; that of tongues must not be refused; the principle of order must prevail in the life of the Church, and each man in his turn and place must use the gifts that God has given him therein.

VIII

THE RESURRECTION OF
THE BODY

15.

There are several points to remember about the doctrinal chapter which now confronts us. First of all, although it is the classical New Testament exposition of the subject, it must not be studied in isolation, but in connection with other statements about it, scattered about in St Paul's epistles (as, for example, in I Thess. 4.13-17; I Cor. 6.14; II Cor. 5.1-4; Rom. 8.11; Phil. 3.21) and references elsewhere in the New Testament, notably Mark 12.25-27 and John 11.23-27. As the opening verses of this chapter show, St Paul was dealing with something that was part of the common Christian heritage. Next, he was dealing with a subject in which he was on common ground with much Jewish and Greek teaching. Undefined as it was, there was in both cultures a general acceptance of some idea of immortality. But, next, it must be remembered that there was a difference between the Jewish and Greek approaches to the subject, a difference which was directly concerned with their thought about the body. For the Hebrew ' man does not *have* a body, he *is* a body ';[1] ' there is no suggestion that the soul is the essential personality, or that the soul is immortal, while the flesh is mortal.' On the other hand, to the Greeks the soul was everything, and was by its very nature immortal. The body was at best a hindrance and at worst evil, always something to be escaped from; death gave to the soul release from a prison-house. Fourthly, we

[1] Robinson, p. 14.

have to remember that when St Paul refers in this chapter to the body there are in his mind all the different aspects of that word as it presented itself to Hebrew thought which we have already seen in this epistle. Not only is he thinking of the body as something essential to a whole personality, which can be represented as a whole by almost any part of it: he is also thinking of the body as that which, far from securing for a man his separateness from his fellows, is actually that which makes him part of humanity as a whole, so that he never stands in the presence of God as one 'alone with the Alone' but as one amongst his fellows, a social personality and not a solitary individual. Hence, when St Paul speaks of the body he never has far from his mind the Christian as a living part of Christ in his Body, the Church; it is in this corporate setting that he sees the individual Christian from baptism to resurrection. Behind this line of thought is the idea of the solidarity of the whole human race. 'Adam' is the head and representative of it, and St Paul argues from this familiar concept to the solidarity of the Christian community IN CHRIST; we read, AS IN ADAM ALL DIE, EVEN SO IN CHRIST SHALL ALL BE MADE ALIVE.

All this is part of the background to ch. 15, and it is important that we should see what it is that the Apostle is concerned with here. He is not arguing for any doctrine of the immortality of the soul; such a doctrine is completely absent from the New Testament, in which in fact the word 'immortality' occurs only twice, once in this chapter (v. 54) and once at I Tim. 6.16. The points at issue were whether a future life, which as we have seen was common ground to both Jews and Greeks, entailed a resurrection, and whether there was any sense in which the body could be thought of as sharing in this future life. There seems to have been little or no questioning of the fact of the resurrection of Christ: the difficulty was that some Christians could not see that the resurrection of the dead followed from it. It could, for instance, be argued that what the resurrection meant for Christians was their sharing in the risen life of Christ, which was brought about as a consequence of their baptism, and that the resurrection was therefore a past event. See, for example, the expressions we find in Col. 2.12: YOU WERE BURIED WITH HIM IN BAPTISM, IN WHICH YOU WERE ALSO RAISED WITH HIM THROUGH FAITH IN THE WORKING OF GOD WHO RAISED HIM FROM THE DEAD (RSV). Such may have been the views put forward later by Hymenaeus and Philetus (II Tim. 2.18). What the Corinthians had to learn was the full meaning of the resurrection of Christ. First of all it was to be seen in the decisive event of Easter Day, which was part of the apostolic proclamation of the MYSTERY now to be given to all the world; next it was to be seen in baptism, baptism into the Holy Spirit, alike of the Church at Pentecost, and on the baptismal day of each individual Christian when he is incorporated into the risen life of Christ by being made a MEMBER OF CHRIST, a living part of his Body, the Church. For such a one, although 'the natural phenomenon of physical death must still take place, the mortal crisis of spiritual death and judgment is a thing of the past. Henceforth they are alive unto God in Christ Jesus.'[1] This comes about because the resurrection of Christ was not just the raising to life of an individual man; for Christ was not just a man, but Man, in whom the whole human race, in virtue of its solidarity and his representative capacity, 'in principle triumphed over death'.[2] Finally, this experience of the risen life in the Spirit is, as the Fourth Gospel says of eternal life, something which has not only a present but a future reference. Their present experience of NEWNESS OF LIFE in the Church is indeed the guarantee of the fullness of life which awaits them in the Parousia (see II Cor. 1.22 and 5.5, where the word translated 'earnest' or 'pledge' is a Semitic word arrabon, a part given

[1] Alan Richardson, 'Resurrection', TWBB, p. 195.
[2] TWBB, p. 195.

in advance of what will be bestowed fully afterwards).[1]

In this resurrection life, St Paul had further to show, the body was necessarily involved, for he was A HEBREW OF THE HEBREWS and for him there could be no question of a 'whole man' apart from his body. It was here that his chief difficulty lay so far as these new Gentile Christians were concerned, for such an idea was wholly alien to their thinking. His answer to their problem lies in a frank rejection of cruder Jewish ideas of a resurrection of the flesh in any literal sense (he has already implied this in I Cor. 6.13); FLESH AND BLOOD CANNOT INHERIT THE KINGDOM OF GOD (v. 50). But there will be a change of substance both for the living and the dead when the Son of Man comes in his glory; the body will still be involved, but it will be a body suited to the fullness of the resurrection life.

All this did not mean that the Apostle based his teaching about the resurrection on philosophical or speculative theories. He bases it upon the fact of the resurrection of Jesus, which he sees as the culmination of that divine plan which resulted in the series of divine acts which began with creation. It is to be grasped in all its significance by faith, and the natural sphere in which that gift of the Spirit is to be expected is within the redeemed community, the Christian Church; where hope, too, will have its place, hope which looks forward to the full enjoyment of the 'glorious liberty of the children of God'; where the guarantee and foundation of everything is seen in the understanding of the nature of God himself in terms of love, of charity.

THE RESURRECTION OF CHRIST

15.1-11

1-3. Here the Apostle repeats what he had already claimed

[1] See Moulton and Milligan, p. 79, where the meaning is fully illustrated from the papyri.

more briefly in 4.15. His bringing to them the Good News
puts him in a special relationship of love to them; he is, in
a special sense, their father-in-God, and as such deserves
their complete confidence. His claims are, moreover, supported by their own experience of what, as a consequence
of his preaching and their acceptance of it, salvation means.
What he preached was not in any sense 'his' gospel; it is
the gospel which he shares with the Church, from whom he
received it.

4-7. In these verses we can no doubt see the way in which
creeds originated; they were almost like hymns—easily
remembered rhythmical sentences in which great truths
were recited at public worship. The statement of the
'scheme of salvation' here is by no means complete and
is not meant to be, any more than the list of witnesses to
the resurrection is meant to be exhaustive. The 'saving
acts' immediately relevant to his purpose are selected, and
the witnesses named are either those already known to the
Corinthians or people about whom information was not
difficult to get.

4. Two references to THE SCRIPTURES at the very beginning
of the statement emphasize the divine plan behind the events
which he recites. We have here one of the indications of the
existence from the Church's earliest days of a collection
of proof-texts. Passages that would on this occasion be used
would no doubt include Isa. 53 and Hos. 6.2.

5-7. the twelve . . . all the apostles
These words are a clear illustration of the special official
status of the apostolic body, even though there were but
ten present on this occasion. They are 'the original nucleus'
(Harnack) and they form the link between the new Israel
and the old, symbolized by the twelve tribes, even though

this ceased to be a numerically accurate term at an early date. But despite their official status the Apostolate was not confined to the Twelve.

We know nothing from the canonical Gospels of any appearance TO JAMES or even which James was meant, but probably it was JAMES, THE LORD'S BROTHER, an appearance to whom is mentioned in the apocryphal *Gospel according to the Hebrews*.

8. he was seen of me also

it is to be noted that the verb used for this is the ' seen ' used of the pre-ascension appearances to the others. St Paul has no doubt that he has himself seen the risen Lord; the intensity of his conviction of this dominated his life. His conviction of the depth of his sin against Christ, and the suddenness of his conversion, lead him to describe himself as ' the ABORTION of the apostolic family '. Owing nothing to his own powers he is kept alive by the free love (grace) of God, to whom he owes everything. Even though his apostolic claims might seem to be supported by more than apostolic labours, yet it was God's call and God's free grace, all undeserved as it was, that provided the only true foundation for his claims (v. 10). But whoever it was who proclaimed it, it was the same gospel, the gospel which the Corinthians had received from him.

CONSEQUENCES OF DENYING THE DOCTRINE OF THE RESURRECTION

15.12-19

It is possible that some Corinthian Christians doubted or denied the resurrection of Christ; certainly they must have had many pagan friends who did. It is for such people that the evidence at the beginning of this chapter is summarized. But the real problem lay with Christians who accepted the fact of Christ's resurrection and regarded it as a single unique event which proved nothing as to the rest of mankind or could be held quite rightly together with the acceptance of some kind of doctrine of the immortality of the soul. What they have failed to see is the centrality and vital necessity of this event for the whole Christian life, and of the place of the body in it. It is the raising of the Second Adam, the New Man, from death to life; into this New Man Christians have been incorporated at baptism; they have been buried with him in baptism; but their baptism was not baptism with water only, but with the Spirit. In the Spirit they live within the Church and share the risen life of Christ in his Body the Church, which receives life from the Spirit of him who raised up Jesus from the dead. Hence the resurrection of Jesus cannot be treated as an isolated event; it is vitally linked with the whole life of the Christian community. In that community by union with the risen Christ the power and penalty of sin are both done away; DEATH HAS NO MORE DOMINION over them (Rom. 6.9). This they have known and experienced. But they have only known this because they have known the resurrection of Christ. Now Christ was not a man, but Man, and we cannot separate his humanity from the humanity of the rest of mankind. If our bodies are not fit to share in the future life then Christ cannot have risen, for his body was in no way different from ours. If Christ is risen, dead men can rise and look forward to the fullness of life which awaits us all. If dead men cannot rise, then Christ is not risen, and if this be true the whole Christian scheme is shown to be a complete delusion, the experience of salvation merely imaginary and the Apostles guilty of false witness about God and his nature.

CHRIST'S RESURRECTION ASSERTED AS PART OF THE DIVINE PLAN

15.20-28

20. the firstfruits

Commentators have often pointed out that taking Nisan 16 as the probable day of our Lord's resurrection we have the day when the first-ripe sheaf was dedicated to God in token of the dedication to him of the whole harvest. So Christ's resurrection symbolized the resurrection of all believers. It is unlikely that St Paul is here thinking of the redemption of all humanity. The whole context is concerned with Christians, with the Church, although we cannot finally rule out here, any more than we can in Rom. 11. 25-36, for example, the possibility that he has in mind universal redemption.

21. since by man came death

Death to the Christian is an enemy; to the pagan it is a blessing, releasing the immortal soul from its bodily trappings and hindrances. St Paul's thinking is based on Gen. 2 and 3. Death was in the world before man, but it is only through Adam's choice that death becomes the penalty for sin, for wrong deliberately chosen and good rejected. St Paul sees Adam, as we have noted already, as representative man; we are all, as it were, involved in him, for death.

22. So Christ in his turn becomes the new representative man; we are all, as it were, involved in him, for life.

23. each in his own order

Here we have, in the divine plan itself, the ground for that ORDER which St Paul has demanded again and again in this epistle.

K

Christ the firstfruits

First of all in the sense that we have seen above (v. 20), but also in the setting of the expectation of the End that was so constantly in the minds of these early Christians. Even the risen life which all Christians are experiencing in the Body of the Church, in other words, in Christ, is but a foretaste, essentially and necessarily only a partial experience, of that which is to come.

24. deliver up the kingdom to God, even the Father

A difficult phrase, but we must think of it in terms of Christ's work as the completion of the divine purpose in the establishment in God's world of the rule of love.

all rule and all authority and power

This may mean nothing more than an emphasizing of the completeness of the sovereignty of God now established, but in view of the reference to ENEMIES in the next two verses we shall more probably be right in seeing here a reference to those spiritual evil influences and powers to whom St Paul ascribed this world's darkness, and amongst whom he seems at times almost to personify sin and death (cf. also Rev. 17.13 f.; 19.15).

25. He sees the spiritual guarantee of this triumph in the prophecy of Ps. 110.1 and (v. 27) Ps. 8.6. Both these psalms, especially 110, were quarries for Messianic proof-texts, and were regularly so used by the Church. (Cf. our Lord's own use of Ps. 110 in Mark 12.35-7.) St Paul, following tradition, sees the Messianic reign as preparing the way for the final triumph of God and his people; but here he identifies it with the Church, the New Israel, in whose resurrection life death's victims are all rescued and DEATH IS ABOLISHED.

27 f. After quoting Ps. 8.6, HE PUT ALL THINGS IN SUBJECTION UNDER HIS FEET, St Paul adds the remainder to these verses to make clear that the work of Christ is part of the divine plan and cannot be thought of apart from that plan. Christ's whole work is directed to restoring the broken communion between God and man. (Cf. II Cor. 5.18: THIS, AS ALWAYS IS GOD'S DOING; IT IS HE WHO, THROUGH CHRIST, HAS RECONCILED US TO HIMSELF: Knox.) 'Now we see God and experience his action through the God-man, who represents him to us; then Christ will have brought us to the Father; we shall enjoy the Beatific Vision and immediate union with God himself' (Goudge on 15.28).

FURTHER IMPLICATIONS OF UNBELIEF

15.29-34

The Apostle turns back to the general argument with the Corinthians; their day-to-day life as Christians takes the resurrection for granted.

29. baptized for the dead

We have no clue to the meaning of this obscure and difficult verse, which may refer to nothing more than 'an eccentric aberration' on the part of the Corinthian Church.[1] Commentators see a parallel in the sacrifices offered by Judas Maccabaeus on behalf of Jews fallen in battle (II Macc. 12.43-5). The least unlikely explanation is that some Corinthians were ready to be baptized for the eternal good of their friends who had died before being able to secure baptism for themselves. But this is only a guess, and the one thing clear is that some Corinthians followed a baptismal practice which St Paul is able to point out would have been meaningless if they had not believed in a resurrection of the dead.

[1] See a letter from Professor R. H. Fuller in *Theology*, July 1956.

31. Translate with Knox: I SWEAR TO YOU BY ALL THE
PRIDE I TAKE IN YOU IN THE NAME OF OUR LORD JESUS
CHRIST, THAT DEATH IS DAILY AT MY SIDE.

32. This can hardly be taken literally, in view of the
omission of such an event from the list of his experiences
given in II Cor. 11.23 ff., and of the unlikelihood of a
Roman citizen appearing in the arena in a combat of such
a kind, particularly in a provincial centre. It is a powerful
metaphor describing what he has suffered at men's hands,
possibly with a memory of the violence of the mob at
Ephesus (Acts 19.28-34). See, too, 4.9-13 of this epistle
for a picture of what he has in mind.

let us eat and drink

A view of life expounded in Wisd. 2.1-9; but he is
probably thinking of the Jews in Isa. 22.13 who turned
their backs on the warnings of the prophets with these
words.

The criticisms directed at St Paul's moral teaching in
connection with these verses miss the point. He is not discussing the relationship between religion and morals; he
is concerned to assert that without the Christian revelation,
apart from Christ, life has no meaning for him. Ethical
standards had been set before him in the Jewish Law and
he had known nothing but a sense of frustration and bewilderment. His surrender to Christ had meant a totally
different view of life and its significance; he could no longer
think of it except in fellowship with the living Christ, and
that meant, and must mean, a fellowship which death could
not break, or it meant nothing at all.

33 f. With the aid of a tag from the comic poet Menander
he ends this short paragraph with a warning that the attitude
of mind he has been considering has its dangers and should
be shunned. Ignorance of God and his ways is what it

reveals, despite the boast of those who possess it that they are the possessors of 'knowledge' (cf. chapters 2 and 3).

THE NATURE OF THE RESURRECTION BODY

15.35-49

35-41. We must remember that St Paul is here dealing in illustrations from and looking for analogies in the natural world which will throw light on the supernatural event which he is discussing; exact correspondence in detail will be looked for in vain, and under pressure the analogy will break down. (For example, sin has no place in the death and transformation of the seed). But the points which he is concerned to make in these verses are made through these illustrations: he shows that there is biological continuity in the process from death to life, and that the life into which the seed is transformed is a richer and fuller one. He also wishes to emphasize the sovereignty of God throughout the whole process, and to meet the difficulty about WHAT KIND OF A BODY? by calling attention to the infinite variety of the natural order, all of which is created by God.

37. The THOU is emphatic in the Greek, as against GOD in v. 38.

42-49. We pass from the illustrations and analogies to the truth with which we are concerned.

44. a natural . . . a spiritual, body
The first Greek adjective, *psychikon*, means here roughly what we mean by physical life, a body fitted for existence on the material plane; the second, *pneumatikon*, means a body which is spiritually controlled and is fitted for existence on the spiritual plane (cf. 2.14 and note on 10.4).

45. It is this verse which contains the heart of the matter. Man does not sin alone and he will not be glorified alone. His existence is always a corporate one. We share the common nature of all humanity; as such we live on the physical level; but within this life there is a principle akin to the life of God himself, in virtue of which, through the power of the life-giving Spirit, we can be raised to share in that divine life. God's gift of life has made man a living soul, through the life we share with THE FIRST MAN, ADAM. With THE LAST ADAM, the Christ, we enter on a new way of life, which we receive from him who creates the new life as he did also the old (8.6). 'The new creation, which is signified by the term: "last Adam", exists in the incarnate Lord. The Son of God became the anointed man upon whose human spirit rest all the gifts of the Holy Spirit in their fulness. . . . By being joined to him as members of the One Body we become partakers of his Spirit-anointed life. . . . We begin to bear in our spirits the image of God's Son, which we shall hereafter bear manifestly in our risen bodies (v. 49).'[1] Cf. II Cor. 5.15-18: CHRIST DIED FOR US ALL, SO THAT BEING ALIVE SHOULD NO LONGER MEAN LIVING WITH OUR OWN LIFE, BUT WITH HIS LIFE WHO DIED FOR US AND HAS RISEN AGAIN; AND THEREFORE, HENCEFORWARD WE DO NOT THINK OF ANYBODY IN A MERELY HUMAN FASHION; . . . WHEN A MAN BECOMES A NEW CREATURE IN CHRIST, HIS OLD LIFE HAS DISAPPEARED, EVERYTHING HAS BECOME NEW ABOUT HIM. THIS, AS ALWAYS, IS GOD'S DOING (Knox).

47. the second man is from heaven

The thought is of the Second Advent rather than of the Incarnation.

[1] Thornton, p. 275.

WHAT OF CHRISTIANS WHO SURVIVE UNTIL THE SECOND COMING?

15.50-58

Briefly, the answer is that what is true of the dead must be true of them. 'A body conditioned by *psyche* (physical, material), derived from Adam, will be transformed into a body conditioned by *pneuma* (spiritual), derived from Christ';[1] cf. Phil. 3.21: HE WILL RE-MAKE THE BODY THAT BELONGS TO OUR LOW ESTATE TO BE LIKE HIS OWN GLORIOUS BODY.

50. flesh and blood

Here this phrase simply means our physical nature and not what the Catechism calls 'the sinful lusts of the flesh'.

51. a mystery

This still has the sense, though here more restricted, of a special revelation he has been commissioned to make.

The Latin versions here have a different text which would translate as 'We shall all rise again but not all of us will undergo the change I speak of' (Knox), but this reading is due to misunderstanding of what St Paul wrote. His concern is with those who were puzzled as to what was to happen to Christians who were still alive at the Second Coming, and the verse is an explanation of the previous one.

52. One living in the nuclear age may be forgiven for pausing to note that the Greek word translated here 'a moment' is also the word for 'atom', and that the whole phrase can be equally well translated: 'by an atom'.

---

[1] ICC, note on 15.48 f.

at the last trump

St Paul uses the common apocalyptic imagery. Earlier (14.8) he has spoken of the confusion caused in an army when THE TRUMPET GIVES AN UNCERTAIN SOUND; here, obeying as it were no uncertain signal, living and dead will meet the risen Lord (cf. I Thess. 4.16), EACH IN HIS OWN ORDER.

53. See II Cor. 5.1-4 for what might almost be called a commentary on this verse. The passages are not contradictory, for the II Corinthians passage, like this one, emphasizes the continuity between this body and the body of the resurrection. In both passages the soul *and* the body are involved, and in II Corinthians it is at least possible that THE BUILDING MADE WITHOUT HANDS, ETERNAL, IN THE HEAVENS is the Body of Christ, the Church, in which both the living and the dead are incorporated by baptism.[1]

54 f. St Paul combines and adapts Isa. 25.8 and Hos. 13.14 (LXX) to celebrate the final triumph, the annihilation of death, and God's universal reign.

56. For the expansion of the thought THE STRENGTH OF SIN IS THE LAW see Rom. 5.12-21 and 7.1-13, where he suggests that we owe to the Law our recognition of right and wrong, and also that its forbidding of the latter so affects our perverse nature as to rouse in us a determination to indulge in it.

58. Moffatt (p. 269) quotes Aristotle, *Nichomachean Ethics* 2.4, to explain what St Paul means here: 'In the case of moral excellence a man must know what he is doing, then he must choose to do it for its own sake, and finally his action must express a stable, immovable character.'

---

[1] See Thornton, pp. 284 f., and Selwyn, *I Peter*, Note H, pp. 289 f., for a full treatment of this passage.

IX

THE LETTER CONCLUDED

16.

THE COLLECTION FOR POOR CHRISTIANS
AT JERUSALEM

16.1-4

After this tremendous chapter, the epistle ends on a note of quiet, even, it seems at first sight, of bathos. NOW ABOUT THE COLLECTION FOR THE JERUSALEM CHURCH, writes the Apostle. We feel rather as we do when Vergil, after describing Dido's last passionate and agonized reproaches hurled at her false lover, and raising us to the height of tragedy, resumes his narration with the words '*At pius Aeneas. . . .*'—'But Aeneas, ever the slave of duty. . . .'. But this is to mistake the Apostle's attitude to this collection. It was very much a 'concern' of his. What seems to have been chronic poverty at Jerusalem would have been aggravated for converts to Christianity (*a*) by their ceasing to be eligible for the well-organized Jewish poor relief, and (*b*) probably by the pooling of goods referred to in Acts 4.32. There was therefore an immediate and very practical reason for St Paul's concern. But such relief would also be an effective witness to Jewish Christians both of his loyalty to what one might call 'the mother-church' and of the effectiveness with which he was able to use his own apostolic authority. It also emphasized to his converts the reality of their common membership in the Body of Christ, and

153

was an obvious illustration of his teaching in ch. 12 of this epistle: IF ONE MEMBER SUFFER, ALL THE MEMBERS SUFFER WITH IT. (For other references to the collection, see also II Cor. 8-9; Rom. 15.26; Gal. 2.10; Acts 24.17.)

1. I gave order
The Greek word is a very authoritative one, and indicates the respect which St Paul's apostolic office received.

The churches of Galatia
i.e., those referred to in Acts 13-14, namely Antioch, Iconium, Lystra and Derbe, cities in the Phrygian region in the Roman province of Galatia, or South Galatia.

the saints
Once again, the best translation is simply ' the Christians '.

2. on every first day of the week
It is interesting that our earliest example of the revolutionary change indicated by the substitution of Sunday for Saturday as the principal Christian day of worship should follow so closely on a passage dealing with the resurrection, to the truth of which it is one of the most significant indirect proofs.

It is a loss to the Church that the methods of Christian giving the Apostle here commends have not become established. Giving is to be regular, unhurried, related to one's profits, properly administered by responsible persons.

INTENDED VISITS BY PAUL, TIMOTHY AND APOLLOS

16.5-12

5-9. These verses show St Paul's affection for his Corinthian converts, despite the faults he has to find with them;

they make the later outbreak of hostility towards him seem
very much the work of a small group, possibly even of
newcomers or visitors to the church there.

7. to see you by the way
   i.e., ' I want to have more than just a passing glimpse of
you.'

9. Acts 19 provides evidence of the accuracy of St Paul's
summing up of the position in both directions.

10-12. Probably neither of these proposed visits took place
for, as we learn from Acts 19.22, Timothy had to go through
Macedonia, and St Paul was anxious to have him back
again (v. 11), which might well have made it impossible to
get to Corinth. As for Apollos, he was evidently firmly
convinced that a visit from him now would do no good,
and we never hear of him again.

10. see that he be with you without fear
   i.e., do make him feel completely at home with you.
Much the same words might be addressed by a bishop to a
modern parish expecting a nervous young deacon!

12. These words serve to show both the close relationship and confidence between St Paul and Apollos and also
to make it plain that the refusal to come was entirely the
decision of Apollos himself.

FINAL SALUTATIONS AND EXHORTATIONS

16.13-24

13 f. Perhaps the letter was originally intended to end here
with these final short pregnant words, containing in them-

selves so much of what the whole epistle had been concerned with; in particular v. 14 means 'more than that,
everything they do must be accompanied with love; love
must be the very atmosphere in which their lives move'
(ICC, p. 304).

15-18. Having mentioned his own helpers, the Apostle
turns to those who from Corinth itself have done so much
to establish the Church there. What they have done requires
the Corinthians to offer them due reverence and to look to
men like them for guidance in their problems when the
Apostle himself is not with them.

A PROPHET IS NOT WITHOUT HONOUR SAVE IN HIS OWN
COUNTRY seems to have been a true proverb so far as
Corinth was concerned, and half a century later Clement
of Rome found them much the same.

19-24. From himself and from their own people the
Apostle now passes to Christians in other parts of the
Church, thus reminding the Corinthians, as he so often had
occasion to do in his correspondence with them, that they
are part of a whole, that *their* church exists because *the*
Church does.

19. Asia
i.e., the proconsular province of that name.

20. a holy kiss
like the 'Amen' this Jewish custom passed into the use
of the Church and we may well have here a mention of
something which was already part of the liturgy like the
prayer MARAN ATHA. Moffatt thinks the custom derived not
from Judaism but from Roman social custom, where the
family kiss was specially emphasized. By the time of Justin
Martyr it was established as a regular liturgical act.

21-24. Concluding exhortations, in keeping with the main burden of the letter, added in the Apostle's own hand, as for the Galatians and for the Thessalonians, and recognizably his own LARGE LETTERS, a sprawling handwriting perhaps, due to his sufferings or possibly to bad eyesight, on one possible interpretation of THE THORN IN THE FLESH to which he refers in Gal. 4.13-15; II Cor. 12.1-10.

22. anathema

let him be banished from the Lord's presence.

Maran atha

almost certainly, in the light of Rev. 22.20, a prayer COME, LORD. From the early Christian manual, the *Didache* or 'Teaching' (? mid-second century), we learn that it was regularly used as the *agape* or fellowship-meal passed into the Eucharist. Cullman sees it as 'above all a eucharistic prayer' and comments: 'The fact that this prayer is handed down by Paul untranslated and that it continued in that original form until the time of the composition of the Didache shows the extraordinarily important rôle which this oldest liturgical prayer of the early Christian community must have played.'[1] Thus the epistle ends as it began (1.7), with the thought of the expectant Church, eagerly awaiting the Coming of the Lord.

[1] Cullmann, *ECW*, pp. 13 f.